A GARDENER'S GUIDE TO

NATIVE PLANTS OF BRITAIN AND IRELAND

Rosemary FitzGerald

THE CROWOOD PRESS

First published in 2012 by
The Crowood Press Ltd
Ramsbury, Marlborough
Wiltshire SN8 2HR

www.crowood.com

British Library Cataloguing-in-Publication Data
A catalogue record for this book is available from the British Library.

ISBN 978 1 84797 309 2

Typeset by Simon Loxley
Printed and bound in Singapore by Craft Print International Ltd

CONTENTS

Dedication

To Edith Rawlins who gave me Latin names, and my grandmother
Alice Kavanagh who gave me gardens.

Acknowledgements

Heartfelt thanks to Alice Boyd, Andy Byfield, John David, my sister Nesta
FitzGerald, Liz MacDonnell, Martyn Rix; for company in fields and gardens
(then and always), for information and comments, and for never-ending
botanical chat. Specific thanks to Bob Gibbons and Malcolm Pasley for the skills,
artistry and immeasurable kindness which made the illustrations possible.

Picture credits

Bob Gibbons (Natural Image): p.12 Daffodils (right); p.18 Daffodils; p.19 Cornish
cliff flora; p.20 Moschatel; p.21 Bugle; p.26 Pasqueflowers; p.29 Thrift (above);
p.32 Lily-of-the-valley; p.33 Mezereon (below); p.34 Mezereon, Spurge-laurel;
p.44 Bluebell; p.45 Bluebells; p.48 Daffodils; p. 49 Daffodils;
p.50 Star-of-Bethlehem; p.51 Wood-sorrel; p.53 Solomon's-seal;
p.57 Narrow-leaved Lungwort; p.60 Buttercups; p.65 Daisy (below, right);
p.66 Alternate-leaved Golden-saxifrage; p.70 Wild Tulip; p.74 Lady's-mantle;
p.75 Alpine Lady's-mantle (top, left), Marsh-mallow (bottom, right);
p.79 Clustered Bellflower; p.80 Spreading Bellflower; p.81 Rosebay Willowherb;
p.86 Cheddar Pink; p.87 Maiden Pink; p.89 Teasel; p.95 Meadow Crane's-bill;
p.96 Wood Crane's-bill (top left); p.98 Yellow Horned-poppy; p.102 Oxeye
Daisy; p.105 Sweet Cicely; p.106 Bistort; p.107 Mouse-ear Hawkweed;
p.108 Fox-and-cubs; p.109 Hoary Plantain (above); p.110 Meadow Clary;
p.111 Wild Clary; p.112 Biting Stonecrop (above); p.113 English Stonecrop
(above); p.114 Roseroot, Orpine; p.119 Dark Mullein, Aaron's Rod; p.120 Wood
Vetch; p.127 Chamomile (above, and inset); p.131 Meadowsweet, Dropwort;
p.132 Dropwort; p.133 Field Scabious (below); p.134 Hoary Stock (right);
p.136 Yellow-rattle (above); p.137 Saw-wort (below); p.138 Cornish Moneywort;
p.140 Salsify (left); p.142 Traveller's-joy; p.143 Butcher's-broom;
p.145 Traveller's-joy; p.146 Meadow Saffron; p.154 Ivy; p.160 Privet; p.163 Bird
Cherry (left); p.165 Rosa sherardii (above); p.166 Burnet Rose; p.167 Butcher's-
broom; p.168 Pussy-willow (left); p.171 Elder (top); p.175 Wayfaring-tree;
p. 176 Guelder-rose. Peter Wilson (Natural Image): p.104 Musk Mallow.
BSBI: p.43 Bluebell (below). Midgley & Lilley: p.9 Sweet Violet; p.25 Wood
Anemone; p.31 Lily-of-the-valley; p.37 Snowdrop; p. 140 Goat's-beard (right);
p.158 Gladdons; p.179 Mistletoe. All other photographs are by the author.

FOREWORD

Even before the discovery of America and the arrival from the Ottoman Empire of Tulips, Hyacinths and other bulbs in around 1580, gardens in Britain and northern Europe were filled with interesting flowers, not exotica but local, native species and unusual varieties of them, spotted by observant countrymen and then exchanged between keen gardeners. Few garden plants had travelled very far – red and white Roses, perhaps, from southern Europe, Martagon Lilies, Carnations and Everlasting Peas, as well as some cooking herbs or plants with medicinal uses. Local wild flowers are now seldom seen in garden centres or general nurseries, but many still have a following among discerning gardeners; double Red Campion, red Cowslips or flesh-pink Sweet Violets are some forms of local species which are familiar. Others such as red-flowered Sea Campion or white Harebells are rarities to be searched for and treasured. Not all are unshowy curiosities for the specialist. Some were carefully bred by Victorian clergyman such as the Revd. William Wilks, who spotted a Field Poppy with a pale edge, and from it raised the pale strain called Shirley Poppies, since developed further into 'Angels Choir' and 'Mother of Pearl'. A more recent famous gardener, Christopher Lloyd, saw a bronze-leaved Celandine in a wood near his house at Great Dixter, and brought it into cultivation, calling it 'Brazen Hussey' in honour of his friend from nearby Scotney Castle. White-flowered Ragged Robin was conspicuous in the show gardens at this year's Chelsea Flower Show.

This book suggests all the best wild flowers of Britain and Ireland for gardeners, and discusses their good or sometimes less good qualities. No-one is bet-ter qualified than Rosemary FitzGerald to describe them with authority and from first-hand knowledge, from her childhood listing every wild flower she could find in her Wild Flower Society Field Botanist's Diary, to her work studying rare plants for government conservation agencies in Britain and Ireland and her experience of running her own nursery. She has a deep love and appreciation of these often subtle flowers and her enthusiasm shines through in the writing. It is free from botanical jargon, clear and concise, but often poetic as well, such as when she describes how different flowers grow together in the wild, and how these scenes can be created in the garden.

This book is indispensable for all those who wish to grow wild flowers, whether in a hay meadow, woodland or just in some less cultivated area of the garden; all the flowers are shown here and their individual characters and special preferences are described with the author's quiet confidence.

We can enjoy growing wild plants too, finding them in specialist nurseries and exchanging them with other gardeners. Many can be found through companies that specialize in wild flower seeds, and some even give the origin of the seed they sell, so we can grow ones which originate in the British Isles, and avoid planting central European strains. With a little attention and care, most should then be long-lived inhabitants of our gardens. A group of Summer Snowflakes in a dell at Longleat, praised by William Robinson in the 1870s, is still beautiful today.

Martyn Rix, May 2011

INTRODUCTION

The term 'wild flowers' suggests pretty views and treasured childhood memories; 'weeds' suggests struggle and disorder; 'native species' suggests an academic and scientific view. Of course all these terms describe the same plants, and they don't really contradict each other. The saying that a 'weed is just a wild flower out of place' still holds, and now that 'sustainability' is the key aim of the majority of gardening styles it is an appropriate time to re-assess some of our British and Irish wildlings, and see how some can make a positive contribution to modern gardens. This is not the same thing as 'wildflower gardening', which involves giving much of the available space to mixtures of exclusively wild plants; nor is it 'wildlife gardening', which involves making the needs of birds, insects, amphibians, reptiles and small mammals the gardener's top priority. Growing some native plants will incidentally benefit 'good' insects in particular, but the primary aim of this book is to show how particular wild flowers can make a delightful and well-behaved contribution in quite conventional garden settings, and to explain why others will do precisely the opposite.

The selection has been very strictly made. Plants are recommended only if they have been tried and tested within the garden wall, and if their habits are familiar to the author. Personal choice has been important, and undoubtedly readers will find favourites of their own unfairly left out, or 'weeds' that they dread described as delightful, but gardening styles and wishes are intensely personal, and this book has been designed to suggest rather than to lay down any laws. Looking for either native or garden plants that appeal to your individual taste has much in common with taking part in a treasure hunt, and the species accounts are intended to be the clues. Many of the recommended plants are quite common, or are without specialized needs, so they have a good chance of growing well in most lowland gardens. Plants from bogs, mountains, moorland and other extreme habitats are not included because it is difficult to cater for their special requirements in a more domestic setting.

OPPOSITE PAGE: **Natural gardening – a Cornish cliff in May.**
BELOW: **Sweet Violet – a favourite for centuries.**

Extreme and specialized habitats: (left) cliffs at Mizen Head in Co. Cork; (right) botanists search a dry trackway puddle for a Cornish rarity.

Naturally, this means that some beautiful groups, such as orchids, heathers, gentians and aquatic plants are left out, but all need skills and requirements beyond the scope of most of our 'common or garden' situations. Unlike nursery stock which has been fed and watered to perfection all its life, wild plants have to cope with an extremely tough existence, and often have independent and quirky ways with which the gardener needs to become familiar, so growing the easier ones well is the best way to start making them your friends.

A multitude of strategies have evolved over time to protect plants from threats and enable them to succeed in reproducing. They have to be able to survive drought and flood, being scorched or frozen, having countless hungry organisms try to eat them; and for every second of their existence they have to struggle to compete with other plants for light, water and nutrients. It is hardly surprising that some, put in good garden soil without this fierce competition, are too successful, and become invasive pests.

Like all plants, our wild flowers may be annual – growing from seed to flower to fruit, and then dying, within one year; biennial – germinating from seed one year, usually in summer or autumn, and living through a winter before flowering, fruiting and finishing the next year; or perennial – taking probably two winters before flowering, and then living on, flowering, fruiting and increasing in size for a number of years. They can be evergreen – keeping at least some green leaves during the winter; or deciduous – dying back after flowering, or in the autumn, and keeping their growing parts safe underground during the coldest weather. These very simple basic categories are obviously 'need to know' for gardeners. Plants prefer either sun or shade, dry or damper soil, and as wild flowers have such a hard struggle for existence, coping with competition, predators, exposure and poor soils, they are dependent on having appropriate basic supplies of light and moisture. If you are considering using wild plants in your garden, you are probably already sympathetic to 'going with the flow', growing plants where they do best, and not forcing them to fit a particular planting design. This book explains the needs and habits of a selection of the most rewarding and reliable wild flowers, and in doing this offers ideas or brief suggestions for growing many more.

Wild annuals and wild perennials use different strategies, and these too need to be looked at before a wild plant is introduced to a garden. Each of the recommended plants will have their habits explained, but as a rule of thumb perennials will have very strong root systems, and can often spread vegetatively by runners or offsets. Any gardener who has struggled to get rid of Bindweed, Couch Grass, Ground Elder or Dock will know all about the will to live shown by such plants, and the effectiveness of their strategies. Annuals rely mostly on speedy opportunism, so that they can flower and fruit for much of the year if weather allows (think how Common Chickweed or Groundsel can be flowering and vigorous at Christmas in a mild year), but many annuals can equally stop growing and produce good seed from a tiny 'emergency' plant in a very dry spring or summer. Annuals need bare and disturbed ground to germinate – many of our best-loved flowers such as Poppies were cornfield weeds in historic times, germinating in bare ground after ploughing, and coming up mixed with the crop. This is important to remember, because the modern fashion for 'wildflower meadows' can lead to disappointment. Meadows, in the old-fashioned sense of 'flowery meads', were complex mixtures of grasses and flowering perennials (though they are now often rye grass monocultures). The bright seed packets that show Poppies and Cornflowers, are, or should be, mixtures of annuals. They can make a delightful show for a brief summer season, and can be great in a new garden which is still a building site, giving you a bit of colour from dreadful soil while you concentrate on the house; but making a meadow is a very long-term project, very labour-intensive and very difficult! The famous meadow at Great Dixter was already full of wild plants before the garden was developed, and it has since had more than seventy years of careful management to add to its flowery richness.

Becoming familiar with a modest selection of wild plants, and trying them out as a part of your usual gardening style, makes a lot of sense. If you choose to experiment with perennials, they can initially be plants which are easy to remove if you change your mind. With annuals there is no need to give a whole bed over to a mixture – just one or two species can be used in a more widespread trial. They will self-seed, and indeed this can be a great advantage if you like casual charm. They are usually very easy to pull up, the young plants quickly become familiar when you are weeding, and the chance planting combinations which they give are sometimes delightful.

What is a native plant?

Wild plants in Britain and Ireland have an interesting history, which is very closely bound up with our own. The western edge of Europe was covered by ice many times, and only finally became clear a mere 15,000 years ago. Birds can fly, fish can swim, mammals can trot, and even early humans were surprisingly enterprising travellers, but plants are slow. A 'new' patch of land, thrown up by a volcano or deposited by river sediment, takes a huge amount of time to acquire many plant species. Because we were so severely affected by ice ages, and are so remotely placed at the Atlantic edge of the continent, far from the warmer south and east, there was no chance for masses of plant species to recolonize as quickly as rising temperatures might have allowed. The implications of an island habitat are also important, as plants spread over land – stories about seeds sticking to the feet of birds are usually exaggerated. Great Britain was part of the landmass of Europe when the ice finally went, and the North Sea and Channel were low, boggy ground which before long (in geological time) became mostly water, breaking the land-bridge and leaving us an island. What this means for our variety of wild plants is that many of them had to cross the sea with us, a slow and erratic process, and the combined effects of history mean that, compared to the continent, we have a very small flora. The UK's largest

Plants have always been close to human life, and wild flowers often grow in historic settings: (left) traces of ancient fields on Sherkin Island, Co. Cork; (right) wild Daffodils in a churchyard.

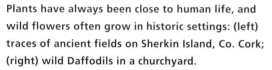

island (England, Wales and Scotland) is nearly thirty times the size of the Mediterranean island of Crete, but Crete has a plant list of about 1,800 species, while ours is smaller, at a mere 1,500 or so.

This strange history does make our little flora interesting though, because it connects us very directly with the past, and with fascinating speculations about how and why some of our wild flowers got here. It could have happened in many ways, as hunters and settlers arrived. The conditions of prehistoric travel often involved bringing animals and their food. Shoes and bedding might have been padded with hay. Boats could have had stones or sand for ballast, which would be thrown out to make space for cargo (both Britain and Ireland were exporting to the continent by 2,000 BC). Farmer settlers will have brought crop seed and plants. There were many, many ways for seeds or root scraps to travel, and enriching the part of our flora that is scientifically accepted as native are a number of plants introduced by people in historic or even prehistoric times. They include some of our best known 'wild flowers', including the Fritillary and Snowdrop. Because they have been here so long, and settled in so well, they are now in a botanical category that acknowledges

their respected status. They are called 'archaeophytes', which indicates that they are ancient introductions, but are not one of the primal species that have been here since the ice. 'Neophytes', newcomers but still well established, are plants introduced after the discovery of the New World (AD 1500). 'Introductions' are relatively recent, many from the last 150 years, and include the notorious Japanese Knotweed.

None of this history is essential information for growing wild flowers successfully in your garden, but because they are so woven into our culture, into art and literature, memory and sense of place, it is interesting to know that they are not all here by chance, but have always shared our lives.

Habitats – wild flowers and where they grow

Because these islands are so crowded now, and have been relatively well-populated since prehistory, there is actually almost no habitat left which has not been influenced by people. Farming, both growing crops and raising domestic animals, has been important for 5,000 years. Woodland has been cleared for farms or managed to produce useful timber. Heaths have been grazed, or heather and furze cut for roofing and bedding. Even wild animals, such as deer, have lived in controlled populations because they have been pro-

tected for sport and food. The most familiar wild creature in Britain, the rabbit, is not native at all but was introduced by the Romans, after AD 43, for fur and meat. So except for an occasional mountain ledge inaccessible to deer and sheep, or an occasional crevice in sea cliffs, humans and their animals have made a mark everywhere.

Plants live in communities, just as we do, and many of our most familiar flowers exist among species which have similar needs and tolerances, and which have adapted to the various ways in which we manage 'natural habitat'. During history, some plant communities have flourished within human management regimes, and knowing a little about how we manage fields and woodland is often the secret to growing wild plants in cultivation. Gardening is after all just miniaturized farming, and it is often surprisingly easy to give common plants just the conditions they need.

Many wild flowers need light and space, and farming processes used to be beneficial: (top) grazing animals kept rank grasses in control; (above) hay used to be cut from established flowery meadows.

WILD FLOWERS AND THE LAW

An important implication of the way our actions influence 'wild' habitats is that every inch (of England at least) belongs to someone, and so do the flowers. Luckily for gardeners very few species are yet rare enough to have the special protection of Schedule 8 of the Wildlife and Countryside Act 1981. Plants on this list are completely untouchable in the wild unless you have a government licence, but the only flowers in the book from this category are *Dianthus gratianopolitanus* (Cheddar Pink) and *Salvia pratensis* (Meadow Clary), both included because they are now widespread in the nursery trade, so easily and safely available. A third species, *Dianthus armeria* (Deptford Pink) can be sourced from seed lists. The Act itself is of course the opposite of light reading, but the important points are straightforward: rare plants must never be touched anyway (if in doubt don't touch), and common plants may only be picked or dug up with the permission of the landowner (the 'authorized person' in the eyes of the law). Many landowners are pleased to be asked about their flowers and can be very kind about allowing small collections for private gardens. Wild material must not be collected for sale. Friends' gardens are a good source of plants, and reputable seed and nursery sources are listed at the end of the book. If you want to look at the wildlife laws in detail you need to plunge into http://jncc.defra.gov.uk; the Plantlife website also has the list of Schedule 8 plants.

Permission is needed to explore, but do ask – many landowners will open the gate.

The peat question

Although plants from highly specialized habitats are not within the scope of this book, one of these habitats has become centre of a controversy involving most gardeners. Peat, an earth-like substance formed by the rotting down of mosses and sedges, mostly during the wet, cold centuries after the ice ages when we had a tundra-like flora, has long been cut for fuel. In historic times this was sustainable, because bog vegetation was forming a little more peat all the time, and demand for cut 'turfs' was limited to the demands of smaller human populations.

But since about 1950 the use of peat has become

unsustainable. Peat-fired power stations in Ireland are consuming the last of the globally unique 'raised bogs', and unfortunately the garden trade has promoted the lower-grade material as an 'essential' compost base and growing medium. Now, big business is stripping virgin habitat in countries such as Estonia, purely for horticultural use. Peat (usually referred to as 'turf' in Ireland) is indeed a useful soil conditioner, and it holds moisture well, but the popular faith in it having magic growing properties is unfounded. Because of the way it is formed (in 'anaerobic' conditions, i.e. without oxygen), peat has no nutrients, which is why peat bogs harbour some of the rare and fascinating plant species that have evolved ways of getting their food by 'eating' insects. The changing climate has almost stopped peat formation, and if our greedy destruction of bogs continues, this amazing habitat and its plants will be lost. All gardeners can

Peat cutting by hand was sustainable. The marks of a special turf spade (known as a 'slane') in a Kerry bog.

support efforts to find the 'peat alternative', and any with organic leanings may want to do this quickly when they consider that all nutrients in peat must be added artificially as chemical supplements.

NAME CHANGE ALERT

An immensely important book was published in 2010. The third edition of Clive Stace's *New Flora of the British Isles* is now the definitive work on the naming and identification of British plants. The book is for use by serious and professional botanists, and is considered to set the authoritative standard of reference for years to come. It is important here because a number of familiar wild flowers have had their names revised, and are now placed in initially unfamiliar genera. To keep the present book as approachable as possible, the 'old' names have been retained, but the 'new' names are given (marked with an asterisk*), and it must be noted that future publications will use the 'new' version.

A word about names

Many people dread the idea of having to use Latin names; they can seem strange, hard to learn, and affected in use, but they are essential to make sure that focus is on the right plant. This is particularly true with wild flowers. Because we have known them throughout history – some grow in all parts of the British Isles – they have collected a multitude of local names (known as the 'common' names). The familiar golden Marsh-marigold of March ditches had more than ninety English names collected by John Grigson for *The Englishman's Flora* (first published in 1958), and some of these, such as 'Bull-rushes', 'Buttercup' and 'May-flower' usually stand for quite different plants. It depends where you were born, where your parents or grandparents were born... in fact it can be really difficult and confusing trying to identify such a plant from its common name only. In Latin, however,

Opposite: **A Sundew,** *Drosera intermedia*, **in a Dorset peat bog. Sticky hairs trap insects which are digested to feed the plant.**

there is only one *Caltha palustris*. The specific name (the second part of the Latin binomial) is often interesting because it is quite literal, and tells something about the plant – '*palustris*' means 'of the marsh' – but some can give more general information. For instance, '*officinalis*' indicates that a plant has had medicinal uses, and used to be on official lists of approved drugs. In this book plants are listed by their Latin names, to make identification certain, but commonly used English names are always given, and the index covers both. This means that the correct species is unarguably named, but there is no dismissal of the familiar and sometimes very ancient and charming common names. Common (or 'English' names) are written in different ways by different people. In this book I have followed the convention used in Clive Stace's *New Flora of the British Isles* and given them capital letters.

Structure of chapters

The chapters follow the order of the seasons: spring, summer, autumn/winter, so plants are identified with the time of their greatest interest and value in the garden year. Some may be associated with more than one season, but this is noted in individual accounts. For instance ferns are included in the summer chapter because that is when their fronds will be finest. Most shrubs are covered in the autumn/winter chapter because of the importance of their leaves and berries, but their flowering times are also mentioned. At the end of the spring and summer chapters there is a list of plants that are not treated in detail, but may

SAVE HABITATS – SAVE PLANTS

Growing wild plants in gardens will not 'save' them in conservation terms as their scientific value (history, adaptations, tolerances) is all locked up in their community and natural habitat. Only by saving the whole package – land, plants and management – can conservation really work. Even in a botanic garden a lone species becomes a museum specimen, a curio. But growing common plants, getting to know them, talking about them, wanting to keep them growing outside the garden as well as inside, can help to secure them a future. Raising awareness is as important now to conservation as it was to feminism in the 1970s, and initiatives such as Plantlife's 2002 'County Flower' survey, when members in England, Scotland, Wales and Northern Ireland voted for a flower to represent their home county, do much to publicize the cause (results are included in the species accounts). The more people there are who know and care about our wild flowers and what is happening to them, the more chance these flowers have of a future. Contact details for organizations concerned with wild plant conservation are given at the end of the book – they welcome new members and have excellent websites and magazines.

be worth testing for use in particular gardens – these have brief notes indicating their needs and qualities.

Rosemary FitzGerald
Somerset
February 2011

SPRING

This is the most important season for using wild flowers in the garden, because their modest beauty shows well when beds and shrubberies are relatively bare, and their colours go prettily among new leaves. A key strategy in the fierce competitive life of a wild plant is to get in first, to take advantage of any spring sun before bigger plants shade it out, to expand its leaves before surrounding foliage crowds in too thickly. In gardens we can take advantage of this early vigour, precisely tuned to the patterns of our climate, and enjoy a whole range of sweet (and often scented) species clothing beds where summer plantings have not yet developed. Many native plants also die back somewhat after flowering, becoming invisible or lurking discreetly among later, larger plants. In the summer, most garden flowers will outshine them, being selected for more showy forms and colours, but the pale lights of spring in these western islands show our natives to perfection.

'Spring' in terms of the flora of Britain and Ireland, is hard to define. Climate and temperature differences between north and south, even between east and west, can be surprisingly large measured by flowering dates. Occasional flowers of Thrift and Sea Campion can usually be found on the coast of Cornwall in January, and Somerset lanes can often show a Primrose for Christmas, but in Scotland the same flowers would still be fresh in June. For this book, spring will cover the months from January to May, and flowering times are based on lowland gardens in England, Wales and the Scottish Border country, and in Ireland.

OPPOSITE PAGE: **Wild Daffodils in Hazel coppice – cutting cycles allow light onto the woodland floor.**
BELOW: **Spring on a Cornish cliff. Bluebells, Spring Squill, Kidney Vetch, Thrift and Sea Campion can all come into the garden.**

The 'clock tower' structure of Moschatel flower heads.

Adoxa moschatellina
(Moschatel, Townhall Clock)

ADOXACEAE *(Moschatel family)*

This odd and enchanting little plant can be found scattered throughout Britain (though not in the north of Scotland, and rarely in Ireland), in shady places with good soil or leaf mould. It is too tiny to be competitive so flowers early, growing in deciduous woodland without thick undergrowth, on hedge banks before coarser species reach full size, and on moist mountain ledges. In the south it can be in flower by the end of March and dies down well before summer sets in. It is perennial, spreading by creeping stolons, and storing energy while it is dormant in little fleshy rhizomes. This leads to dense patches of closely connected plants, only up to about 7cm high, but forming a dainty carpet of scalloped leaves with the green flowers held above on thin upright stems. The name 'Townhall Clock' comes from the unusual structure of the flower head, which has flowers arranged back to

back in a square, a face looking out in each direction (and another right on top).

The other common name, Moschatel, also has an interesting origin, because this modest-looking plant is the only member of its genus, and indeed of its family (which in botanical terms is a 'monotypic family'). The second word of a scientific name (a 'binomial') is known as the 'specific' name, and it distinguishes a plant from its close relatives, doing the same as our Christian names do for us. Here *moschatellina* means 'little musky one', but because this plant has no relatives it can be known simply as the Moschatel. The musky scent of the flowers is not strong, but can be tantalizingly wafted in damp air after rain.

This is an ideal plant for shrubbery, fern bed or shady wild garden – anywhere where you want some delicate green ground cover in April, which can disappear unmissed in May. The best way to establish it is to acquire a clod of soil which contains some rhizomes. Plant this without breaking it up, in nice leafy soil in shade, and hope that it loves your garden and will spread to a larger patch. Moving it in leaf is probably the only practical time, while it is visible, so disturb your clod as little as possible, and make sure that it does not dry out too much in the first couple of weeks. Plant it where you are unlikely to be planting anything else – there is nothing to see above ground except in the spring months, so it is easy to dig it up by mistake during dormancy.

Ajuga reptans (Bugle)

LAMIACEAE, syn. LABIATAE
(Dead-nettle family)

This is a sturdy and attractive little plant, which can be extremely useful, but it does come with a warning: it spreads, very successfully! Its chief method of increase is by runners, which it produces lavishly, and which root at intervals as they travel. Without competition from taller neighbouring plants, or stern control from the gardener, it will form large dense patches at surprising speed. Its advantages are that it is evergreen, will tolerate both sun and quite deep shade, and in flower is most attractive to early bees.

Grown in a sunny situation the leaves take on a range of bronze colours – very attractive because they have quite a shine – and look great with the dark blue flowers. It is a superb ground cover, will tolerate almost any soil (even quite wet), and can be very successful established on a difficult bank where it will bind the soil as well as covering it, or under shrubs where you just want an easy year-round carpet. So a sensible choice of planting place is essential; it is difficult to keep it from swamping weaker species in mixed (e.g. rockery) plantings, and once well-established it is difficult to get out.

Bugle has long been used in gardens. Colour

RIGHT: **Bugle and Celandines. The large flower lips help insects land to collect pollen.**
BELOW: **Bugle runners weave together, rooting to form dense ground cover.**

variation can occur naturally in the wild, so white or pinkish flowers are found occasionally as well as blue, and these forms have been collected by gardeners. The 2010–11 *Plant Finder* lists forty-five cultivars and varieties, with a whole range of flower and leaf colouration. One way to enjoy the plant without getting your garden taken over is to try some of these, because many of them behave less vigorously than the basic species – indeed some with very pale leaf variegation are delicate and difficult. If any of these thrive, grown for ornament rather than pure ground cover, they will all need thinning and dividing at least every other year to keep them unchoked and flowering well. Only one named selection currently has its RHS Award of Garden Merit, and this is the excellent tall form, 'Catlin's Giant' AGM. It does spread, but its dark blue spires look so fine with miniature daffodils or primroses, or rising above the paler blue of *Anemone blanda*, or contrasting with the pointed leaves and flowers of *Erythronium* species, that it is worth working at its management. A more recent selection, sometimes named Black Scallop, is lovely as a seasonal container plant – its gleaming dark foliage makes a good foil for daffodils or tulips, and the Bugle stays safely trapped in the pot!

'Bulbs' of Ramsons on a stream bank, washed clean by flood water.

Allium schoenoprasum (Chives); *A. triquetrum* (Three-cornered Garlic); *A. ursinum* (Ramsons)

ALLIACEAE, subfamily ALLIOIDEAE *(Onion family)*

This is a tale of the Good and the Bad (though not the Ugly).

Our common wild spring garlic, Ramsons, is a familiar sight in many woods, and on hedge banks by country lanes and roads. It sprouts early, sometimes in January in the south, and the smooth matte-green leaves expand to form close clumps, smelling of garlic if bruised. Where the plant is abundant, large expanses of brown woodland floor can become a dense green, turning to dazzling white when the flowers come out in April and May. After flowering, the leaves quickly go yellow and collapse, so by midsummer only an occasional whiff among leaf litter gives a clue to the spectacular spring display. This is a beautiful plant spread out in drifts in the wild, and can safely and deliciously be used in cooking. The florets have a tiny ovary in the centre of each, which tastes of fresh garlic – snipped from the crowded flower head they can be scattered most prettily over soups or salads. The leaves also have the characteristic taste, but lose most of it if overcooked, so it is best chopped raw over vegetables, or added to cooked spinach at the last moment. All in all, it is well worth growing if it can be restrained. Although invisible for much of the year, it can be invasive and dominate areas where it grows. It grows from whitish bulbs which look more like swollen stems than conventional fat bulbs, and it is not unusual to find these in little bunches like some odd fruit, lying where road-

Characteristic drifts of Ramsons flowering in a Somerset wood.

side ditches have been cleaned or banks cut back.

Replanted, they do increase rapidly, so it is a good idea to have it in large pots that can be put out of sight in the shade while it is dormant. Grow it for decoration or as a vegetable; or if you have a shrubbery with principally spring interest Ramsons will carpet it delightfully. It does best in shade or part-shade, in leafy soils that do not get too dry.

The smell is a deterrent for some people, as in full season it will haunt the fur of dogs and cats, or taint the eggs of foraging hens and the milk of grazing stock, and this characteristic contributed to its naming. In Anglo Saxon *hramsa* meant 'rank', and by the time more modern English developed, the same word, *hramsa* (plural *hramsen*) just meant 'wild garlic', as it has done ever since. Many place names, such as Ramsdale, meaning 'wild garlic valley', come directly from the plant name, and it is interesting to find that these historic towns and villages may have inherited this label because of the nasty taste of their spring butter! Many of them still have Ramsons growing commonly in their neighbourhood.

Chives are very much rarer as a wild flower, found

Flowering wild Chives in Cornwall.

Looks aren't everything – Three-cornered Garlic is pretty but invasive.

different colours (there is a delightful compact white form), and letting a number of plants flower instead of snipping them close all the time. There is no need to study its wild habitat before growing it in the garden – all the information is to be found in any herb or vegetable book.

The previous two species are 'good', at least when they are in the right place, but the Three-cornered Garlic is a sad illustration of the sometimes complicated relationship between wild and garden plants. It is not one of our native plants but comes from areas around the western Mediterranean, and is very pretty, taller in flower than Ramsons, with graceful green-striped white bells (it is sometimes called the Cornish Bluebell). It was brought to England in the eighteenth century, and was probably considered a great find – such an easy and delightful spring bulb! However, it quickly jumped the garden wall, being more aggressively invasive than our own Ramsons and colonizing a wider variety of habitats. During the last century in particular it has caused something of an ecological disaster, particularly in the southwest. Though much less well-known than Giant Hogweed or Japanese Knotweed, it too has devastated native vegetation, and is impossible to remove.

Often seen on roadside banks, grassy slopes and at wood edges, it out-competes everything except the rankest grasses and heavy-duty plants such as docks. The leaves come up well before Christmas in southern England and Ireland, and form a dense mat which flops down on other vegetation, choking it and blacking out light, so smaller spring flowers such as Primroses and Violets have no chance. It does eventually die down in summer, but it has effectively stunted any competition right through the first sunny days and the crucial season of spring growth. It is included in this book as a warning about what can happen if gardeners let plants out of their gardens, rather than bringing them in. The species is also shockingly often advertised in bulb catalogues without comment, when it should really have a large label: 'warning – this is a pest'.

only in a few places in Wales, Cornwall and the north of England, but of course the species is one of our most familiar pot herbs, and has been cultivated for centuries. It is found wild all the way round the northern hemisphere, and may be a true native in the UK, though it was probably also brought into their English gardens by Roman settlers, because these people are known to have been very fond of anything tasting of onions or garlic. Wild populations are very variable in flower colour, showing shades from pale pink to quite strong purple, and this can be an advantage in the garden, qualifying Chives as an ornamental as well as for flavour. It is worth searching nurseries for

Wood Anemone – our most frequent 'wind flower'.

Anemone nemorosa (Wood Anemone); *Pulsatilla vulgaris* (Pasqueflower)

RANUNCULACEAE *(Buttercup family)*

County flower of Middlesex: Wood Anemone; Cambridgeshire and Hertfordshire: Pasqueflower

In the garden these two plants have quite different places and uses, but they are very closely related (in strict botanical terms *Pulsatilla* is a subgenus of *Anemone*), and belong to the wonderful range of 'wind flowers' (*anemone* literally means 'daughter of the wind' in Greek) which bring grace and colour to spring gardens, and include the De Caen anemones of the cut flower trade. Many of these come originally from Mediterranean Europe, but the Wood Anemone is widespread in both Britain and Ireland, and the Pasqueflower is known as an iconic, quintessentially English flower. The common name was given by John Gerard in his famous *Herball* of 1597 where he wrote, 'They flower for the most part about Easter (*pasques* in Old French) which hath moved me to name it

Pasque flower, or Easter flower'. It is also known locally as 'Coventry Bells' and 'Danes' Blood', the latter possibly from its presence on ancient defensive earthworks such as the Devil's Dyke and the Fleam Dyke in East Anglia. It is now very rare indeed. Since about 1940 farming has been pushed towards intensive methods, and not only have old pastures been ploughed but even more frequently fertilizer application has changed the complex soil structure and chemical composition of ancient turfs making them unsuitable for some plants – grassland orchids in particular have suffered from changes in soil chemistry. Grazing patterns have also altered as cattle and sheep have been moved to temporary grass leys close to the farm, instead of feeding on rougher, more marginal land, so that former short open swards have become rank or overgrown with bushes, losing their rich flora.

Although they only hang on as a wild flower in Britain in a few protected sites, Pasqueflowers do have an established presence as a garden plant. A number of colour forms including white, red and pink, have been collected by continental nurserymen (the species is more widespread in Europe), and the 'Papageno' range are semi-doubles. The *Plant Finder* always has quite a list, and all the forms are attractive and worth growing, though the rich purple of our English flower is hard to beat.

Creating a slope with the tightly grazed open turf of a wild habitat might not be practicable in a garden, but luckily the plant grows very happily on a sunny rockery, in troughs, or on the edge of a flower bed. It does need good light and good drainage, and likes some lime in the soil (limestone chippings dug in round it will be appreciated). Once established, plants can clump up well, and give a much longer season of interest than just the flowering time – though this in itself can last a couple of months. Stems and leaves have delightful soft silvery hairs, and the seed heads are really beautiful. Perhaps surprising at first sight, *Pulsatilla* actually comes right next to *Clematis* in the buttercup family, and its wonderful feathery seed heads show this. Placing plants above ground level not only helps ensure good drainage, but enables flowers and seed heads to be viewed back-lit by morning or evening sun.

ABOVE: **Pasqueflowers at Barnack Hills and Holes nature reserve in Northamptonshire. The well-drained, rabbit-nibbled grass of these former quarry spoil heaps provides suitable habitat.**
LEFT: **Rich colouring in the English form of Pasqueflower.**

Anemone nemorosa is individually a much less spectacular plant, but it is wonderfully rewarding in the garden if it is grown as is does in the wild, in drifts under trees or tall shrubs, or in the open without taller plants to hide it. It is one of the most widely distributed of our spring flowers, often seen flowering on a sunny day at the edge of woodland, along hedge banks and in coppice clearings, sometimes now on roadside banks where highway management keeps the brambles cut.

Wood Anemones on a Somerset roadside.

The garden Pasqueflower displays the pretty clothing of silver hairs.

It can tolerate deep summer shade, while it is dormant, but in early spring needs light, and its habit of closing its petals and bending its head a little on dark days, but looking wide open up to sunlight shows its preference most gracefully. The whole plant appears dainty, almost fragile, and although it is actually a 'good doer' in the right conditions, it cannot compete for light with more dominant evergreen perennials such as Bugle, so it is good to place it (perhaps with bulbs) in ground that is rather bare in spring, but where taller plants can take over for the summer. Plant it where you are happy for it to fill most of the available space though, because it may do this more vigorously than its frail appearance might predict, and can crowd out other small plants. Like its continental cousins, the blue *Anemone apennina* and *A. blanda*, Wood Anemones also do well in occasionally mown grass under deciduous trees, with small daffodils perhaps or *Crocus tommasinianus*, and following Winter Aconites (*Eranthis* spp.). Roots are widely available. They can be ordered from bulb firms and planted dry, but the disconcertingly thin, thready rhizomes, which have to be planted laid horizontally on soil or compost, can get too shrivelled to be viable if on the shelf too long, and it is probably safer to use fresh material. Many spring plant sales such as those run by Plant Heritage county branches offer good little pots of flowering plants which can be transplanted right away (if you take care not to disturb rooting parts too much). Some colour variation occurs in the wild (pink staining is quite frequent). Many forms have been selected by gardeners, including doubles, and the fascinating 'Bracteata Pleniflora', which has an elaborate ruff of green sterile 'petals' round a white centre. One of the most popular forms is the mild blue 'Robinsoniana' AGM, supposedly found by, and later named for, William Robinson, whose seminal book *The Wild Garden* (1870) gave gardeners the first great alternative to Victorian formality. He praised the Wood Anemone as 'pretty either in its wild or cultivated state', while Robert Gathorne-Hardy in his book *The Native Garden* (1961) named it 'among the sovereign creatures of English spring', and it is still a delight pooled on open grass or among shrubs or ferns.

Pink or blue flowers can occur among wild Wood Anemones.

Armeria maritima (Thrift)

PLUMBAGINACEAE *(Thrift family)*

County flower of Bute, Pembrokeshire and the Isles of Scilly

This charming little plant is one of the most familiar wild flowers in Western Europe, shown on cliffs and rocky shores in countless postcards and guide books. It can be seen flowering in carpets in many coastal areas, and can survive extremes of temperature and exposure.

As well as in its seaside haunts, Thrift is a pioneer plant in other harsh and peculiar habitats. It surprises even experienced botanists when it is suddenly found flowering on high mountains far from the sea – on the Cairngorms and other Scottish mountains it can be found in damp gravelly flushes, or on bare stony ground where a snow patch has melted. It is also one of the few plants that can tolerate soil polluted by 'heavy metals', and flowers merrily (with one of its coastal companions *Silene uniflora*, Sea Campion) on the spoil heaps of ancient lead and copper mines. In

Iceland, where the tundra vegetation on thin soils must be very similar to that which once colonized these islands after the retreat of the ice ages, Thrift, Sea Campion, and Wild Thyme are the commonest of the pioneer species, so they are likely to be amongst our most ancient native plants.

It is ironic then that Thrift is really quite difficult to grow in the garden! Nice soft soils do not suit it. The leaves form a very dense tuft, with a long root beneath, and in its normal fierce habitats the root is often squeezed into a rock crevice, or poked into stony gravel, while the leaf tuft sits on a stony surface. Garden conditions usually mean that the tuft touches cultivated soil, and the whole plant gets waterlogged and rots away. Trial and error can get Thrift established on a rockery, in a gravel bed or rooted between paving stones, but it sometimes means tolerating a series of losses before success. If your garden is windswept and sunny, it is worth persisting, and a number of selections are available from nurseries. Those with white flowers are particularly pretty, and 'Rubrifolia' has delightful beetroot-red leaves. Dead-heading can encourage a few flowers for most of the

LEFT: **Wild beauty – Thrift in full flower.**
BELOW: **Marsh Marigold: 'In early spring the banks are radiant with this common flower, and plants of it stand up out of the dark waters of the ditch'** (Gathorne-Hardy, 1961)

year. The leaf tufts are evergreen and very neat when young, but old clumps are inclined to build up 'trunks' of dead leaves which eventually show untidily, so it is good to keep young plants coming on.

Caltha palustris
(Marsh-marigold, Kingcup)

RANUNCULACEAE *(Buttercup family)*

This plant is a lovely addition to any spring garden that has a pond, stream or boggy place, but it is a true marsh plant and is almost impossible to grow well without year-round wet habitat, and enough space. The glorious shining gold cups of the spring flowers make an exhilarating display on bare ditch or stream edges when summer reeds or sedges are only just shoots.

Later in the summer when surrounding vegetation grows tall, the *Caltha* produces large, coarse leaves and stalks in an effort to gain enough light, and in a

small garden pond this is unsightly. It can be grown with garden plants such as the grand aroid *Lysichiton americanus* (Skunk-cabbage) with its yellow-hooded flowers and later huge leaves, or with other native species such as *Filipendula ulmaria* (Meadowsweet),

The soft mauve of Cuckooflower, set in short grass, makes a pretty addition to the spring garden palette.

Cardamine pratensis (Cuckooflower, Lady's-smock)

BRASSICACEAE, formerly CRUCIFERAE *(Cabbage family)*

County flower of Brecknockshire and Cheshire

This was formerly one of the most familiar of the spring grassland flowers, often seen in masses in damp meadows or hayfields, and by stream sides. During the last fifty years it has decreased because of drainage and the push for 'improved' grassland, which gives high production for grazing, hay or silage, but is based on a few dominant grass species and agricultural clovers and includes almost no native flowering perennials. *Lychnis flos-cuculi* (Ragged Robin), another familiar flower a generation ago, has suffered the same decrease, and this disappearance of 'flowery meads' from lowland damp grasslands is a cultural loss as well as a threat to biodiversity. Cuckooflower can safely be introduced into gardens – it is not an aggressive spreader either by seed or by vegetative increase. The problem is rather the opposite, and it can be tricky to establish. The best strategy is probably to plant it into a grass community as similar to its meadow habitat as possible, where there is already a mixture of herbs and grasses, on a soil that does not get too dry. It needs to be in at least partial sunlight, and not in competition with dominant grasses. *Arrhenatherum elatius* (False Oat-grass), *Dactylis glomerata* (Cock's-foot), *Lolium* spp. (Ryegrasses), are all to be avoided in garden grass seed, together with mixtures that have high percentages of any one *Fescue* or *Agrostis*. The leaf rosettes of Cuckooflower are quite neat and dainty, so not very competitive until well established. Setting mature or plug plants into short spring grass works best, and this very pretty plant is well suited to 'Botticelli' plantings where old-fashioned daffodils are mixed with more modern 'fashion' bulbs like Camassias, to flower in grass which is then left to grow long. Summer meadow flowers can follow on, leaving the main grass-cutting to hay time in July, with no need for further mowing except for a topping in late autumn if

but all of them are strongly competitive and need plenty of space. Bog gardens and stream edges are hard work if you want to keep them tidy, so although native plants such as Marsh-marigold and Yellow Flag (*Iris pseudacorus*) are wonderfully decorative, their use needs careful planning.

grass is still growing. This planting regime was used early last century for orchard grass, with a selection sometimes including red species tulips, and the late-flowering Pheasant's-eye Narcissus, making a romantic show under blossoming fruit trees. The style is well worth considering again now, when low-maintenance plantings are so important.

Double Cuckooflower is occasionally seen in the wild (for some reason, most often in the West of England) and occasionally a curious 'hose-in-hose' form where a tiny second bud grows from the centre of each flower. These can be located through specialist nurseries and plant sales, and are quaint and delightful, but they are easily lost in gardens which get too dry and hot for this plant of cool damp habitat, and it is most satisfactory established in a grassy plot which you want to look meadow-like. In a small garden, where fairly close supervision and care are possible, it is a sweet companion for old primroses, which also detest being baked.

Cardamine is a genus of cresses, and the leaves of Cuckooflower are a very nice fresh addition to sandwiches or salads (though like most wild greens, they seem quite tough compared to the contents of a supermarket salad-bag). Indeed, even the gardener's enemy *C. hirsuta*, the dreaded Hairy Bittercress, tastes perfectly good. If you are not too cross from weeding out yet another crop, making it into sandwiches is quite a pleasant revenge! More seriously, Cuckooflower is an important food plant for the caterpillars of the early-flying orange-tip butterfly, which also collects nectar from the flowers.

Convallaria majalis
(Lily-of-the-valley)

LILIACEAE *(Lily family)*,
subfamily 4 – LILIOIDEAE

Like Chives, this is a native wild plant which we think of as a garden flower, and which is familiar to most gardeners. It comes from semi-shaded banks and deciduous woodland where it gets some winter light,

Lily-of-the-valley spreads by rhizomes.

and is found through most of Britain south of the Scottish border. It grows on differing soils, sometimes on poor and acid sands, at other times found in limestone woodlands and rich leafy soils. It is surprisingly adaptable about light when free from the threats and competitive pressures of life in natural conditions, and its garden habitat does not have to be the same as it is in the wild (normally cool and shady). It is occasionally seen in gardens as a path edging or on a sunny bank doing perfectly well. Garden selections have usually favoured upright forms, with the flowers more visible and showy than on the modestly ground-hugging wild plant. There is a rather bizarre double, one with pinkish flowers and several forms with a stripy cream variegation of the leaves. The latter can be most attractive when the leaves are freshly unrolled, but most become rather dull and dingy in summer. It is really best grown (as it has been for centuries) for the posies of gloriously scented flowers which can be picked from a good patch, and as an adequate shade-tolerant ground cover green till

Wild Lily-of-
the-valley is
low-growing.

autumn. Established colonies can be very long-lasting, and there will always be a supply of offsets for
easy propagation.

Cytisus scoparius (Broom)

FABACEAE, syn. PAPILIONACEAE
(Pea family), tribe 12 – GENISTEAE

County flower of Glasgow

Most native shrubs are included in the autumn–winter section, because their berries and autumn leaves
are so important for the gardener, but Broom has one
great season of glory while it is in flower (which may
be from late April in the south to June in Scotland).
Grigson (1958) calls it 'one of the great landscape
plants' and it can still sometimes be seen flowering in
masses on the poor sandy or gravelly acid soils which
it prefers. It is one of our few native plants to have kept
its own name (Old English *brōm*) throughout history,
and given it to towns and districts. Place names such
as Broomfield are obvious, but Bromley and Bromp-

ton come from the same source, and others are scattered round the country in a similar way to the many
names coming from Ramsons. Another famous historical link is with its early Latin name *Planta genista*. A
spray of Broom pods was the badge of Henry II, and
the plant gave its name to the Plantagenet line of kings.
    Such a luxuriant flower, coming out in the tradi-
tional spring season of love, made Broom popular in
poetic imagery too, and it occurs in traditional ballads
such as *Tam Lin*, *Sheath and Knife* and of course
Broomfield Hill. Sometimes it is used with sad or sinis-
ter undertones, but the plant always has a star part.
'Going down to the Broom' was a common euphe-
mism for slipping away for some courting. Grigson
notes its 'many virtues, amorous, magical, scenic,
medicinal and practical', and Broom has been closely
involved with our lives for many centuries. Sadly, it is
now rather out of fashion in gardens, possibly
because the bushes are not long-lived and need
replacing after four years or so, or possibly because its
real hatred of limy soils has been forgotten, leading to
failed plantings. Using native Broom as a hybrid parent, some wonderful colours were bred and selected
during the first half of the twentieth century, particu-

LEFT: **Defining a landscape – Broom near Aviemore.**
BELOW: **Mezereon – pinkish-purple or white flowers are intensely fragrant.**

larly by the Daisy Hill and Sleive Donard nurseries in Ireland, and some of these are still available, with later good plants like the Dutch-bred 'Boskoop Ruby'. Wild Broom itself occasionally has colour variants, and these are worth growing. 'Andreanus', found in a wild population in the 1880s, has bicoloured crimson and gold flowers, while 'Cornish Cream' is exactly as nice as it sounds. If you have sandy or shaley soil, without lime, and enjoy changes among your shrubs, brooms are beautiful plants for spring borders or sunny shrubberies. After flowering the whippy dark twigs make a pleasant background for summer plantings.

Daphne laureola (Spurge-laurel); *D. mezereum* (Mezereon)

THYMELAEACEAE *(Mezereon family)*

D is for Daphne, Desirable and Difficult! This genus is amazingly popular with gardeners, considering that many of the species are rare, expensive, fussy about

Unusual yellow drupes on a white form of Mezereon.

Sombre beauty – *Daphne laureola* in flower.

soils, inclined to turn up their toes if moved, difficult to propagate... but many of them are also deliciously scented, hardy, and flower in winter or early spring when delight in the garden is in short supply. It is not widely known that we have two native species, both of which make excellent garden plants.

The most familiar of these little shrubs is Mezereon, because like Chives and Lily-of-the-valley, throughout history it has spent as much time inside the garden as out, collected for the pretty pinkish-purple, strongly scented February flowers which cluster tightly on almost bare twigs.

It was also an apothecary's plant, and indeed its odd English name comes from *mazaryun*, the name used by Avicenna (980–1037 AD), an Arabian physician whose writings influenced most of medieval medicine. The berries are poisonous, but the bark was used for centuries in human medicine (though that of Spurge-laurel more frequently for dosing horses). It is now a real rarity as a wild plant, partly because its habitat was among scrub and brushwood which would have been in constant demand for fuel and fencing, and so never had a chance to grow too thick. Wood edges and scrubby marginal land are no longer worked for brushwood and are usually thickly over-grown, so the little *Daphne* has not only been grabbed for gardens, but choked to death in the wild. The berries are taken by birds, and it grows easily from seed, so it is always difficult to define its status as a wild plant. With single bushes in particular, are they bird-sown 'escapes', or a relic of a wild population? Indeed it grows in much of Europe, and seems always to have been rare in Britain, so it may anyway be an ancient traveller rather than a true native. John Gerard grew it in London at the time of writing his *Herball* (1597) but his plant had come from Poland, and there was no record of Mezereon as a British wild flower till 1752, which is considered 'late' in the history of English botany for such an outstanding species. Gilbert White of Selbourne found some a few years later, and wrote of moving it into his garden – a story which must have been replicated many times in different locations. Whatever its history though, it is considered a treasured English wild flower, and is a jewel for the winter garden. It is not long-lived, but will begin to flower in about three years from seed, so if you can save some berries from the birds, it is easy to keep spare plants on the go (just push the berries into a sand and leaf-mould mix; they are 'drupes' with a large seed in a fleshy cover, and germinate quickly). There is a white *D. mezereum f. alba* which has yellow berries – usually they are red – and a few other varieties are available from specialist nurseries.

Daphne laureola, Spurge-laurel, is rather a different plant. It is evergreen – its small bushes with dark shiny leaves do look very like some spurges, in particular the familiar *E. amygdaloides* var. *robbiae* 'Mrs Robb's Bonnet' (a Turkish variant of our own Wood Spurge, brought back from a trip in a keen gardener's hat-box). The flowers are also produced in winter, and are a beautiful clear pale green with yellow anthers, so although the plant has quite a sombre appearance from a distance, close to it is extremely stylish, and goes wonderfully with Snowdrops.

The little bush is usually upright and shapely, the dark leaves looking very good above or among ferns in summer. It is found on the open floor of deciduous woodland on calcareous soils, occasionally in hedges, and will tolerate quite deep shade in summer. As well as in shady rockeries and fern beds, it is worth trying at the edge of a tall shrubbery or copse, with Winter Aconites, Snowdrops, wild Daffodils or 'little blue bulbs' such as *Chionodoxa* spp., which like this winter light/summer shade habitat. It is surprisingly little used in gardens, perhaps because it lacks colour, and unusually among daphnes, barely has a scent. Some people can detect a faint musky fragrance, particularly towards evening, and it attracts early flying insects, but it is certainly not as obvious as

that of Mezereon. Plants are sometimes available from specialist nurseries, and it is worth looking for a continental form *D. laureola* subsp. *philippi*. This has a more prostrate habit, and spreads by runners and by layering itself. It comes from the Pyrenees and tolerates sunlight without scorching, so can be used as a very pleasing shrubby ground cover on banks and rockeries.

Fritillaria meleagris (Fritillary)

LILIACEAE *(Lily family)*, subfamily 4 – LILIOIDEAE

County flower of Oxfordshire

The Fritillary (Snake's-head, Chequered Lily) has real celebrity status among our wild flowers. Images of it flowering in an Oxford meadow, the tower of Magdalen College in the background, are almost universally well known, and water-meadows where it still

The markings on Fritillary flowers suggest some of its picturesque names.

Fritillaries mix well with other bulbs in grass.

flowers in thousands (such as at Cricklade in Gloucestershire and at Stratfield Saye in Berkshire) are now hugely popular nature reserves. Such meadows are now few and carefully protected, because the traditional specialist management of water meadows was abandoned during the last century, and most were drained and ploughed. One would expect that British botanical literature would be full of proud references to this spectacular flower, before modern farming made it a rarity, but like the beautiful Summer Snowflake, which grows in much the same habitat, there are doubts about it being a real native plant. Although in its remaining sites it flowers in thousands, and although as Grigson (1958) pointed out, these sites are very visible in managed lowland meadows near roads, villages, farms and river paths rather than hidden up mountains or on distant islands, nobody recorded the Fritillary 'in the wild' until nearly the middle of the eighteenth century. This is considered very 'late' for such an unmistakable species. Grigson did collect thirty local names for *The Englishman's Flora*, which is usually a sign of a plant being well known for many years, but some are rather generic spring flower names such as 'Crowcup', while others like 'Drooping Bell of Sodom' sound

rather more academic than countrified. Yet another name is 'Guinea-hen Flower' which Gerard (1597) called the plants in his garden (*meleagris* means guinea-fowl, and refers to the speckled feathers). The great herbalist's plants had been sent him from France however, rather than Oxfordshire, and he seemed unaware of it in England. *Fritillaria meleagris* is known across most of Europe, from river flood plains (which would be an almost identical habitat to managed water-meadows), and was much praised in Tudor times as a garden plant, 'greatly esteemed for the beautifieng of our gardens, and the bosomes of the beautiful'.

It seems very possible that the Fritillary may therefore be a seventeenth-century garden escape which found a perfect farmed habitat to move into. Many recorded sites can be associated with big houses, which would have had gardens. Richard Mabey in his wonderful *Flora Britannica* (1996) gives a fascinating profile of the plant and looks at several of the questions about its history, and also at the place it has gained in our art and literature. Arguments still go on among botanists, but native or not, this lovely plant has a special place in the consciousness of both gardeners and wild botanists, and is very worthy addition to any garden. It is widely available from bulb firms, both in its chequered purplish forms and in its subtle 'white on white' form where the markings are barely visible. It can be grown in flower beds or with other bulbs in grass which is later mown, but please remember that its 'wild' habitat in England is damp meadows, often flooded for part of the year, and then cut for hay or hard grazed. In order to flourish Fritillaries need moisture-retaining soils, and surrounding grass needs to be mown in summer or autumn so that it is thin and short when bulbs come through in spring – a build-up of grass litter will choke plants and prevent seeding.

What the craze is about – subtle differences among Snowdrop flowers.

Snowdrops have long been garden favourites.

Galanthus nivalis (Snowdrop)

LILIACEAE *(Lily family),*
subfamily 7 – AMARYLLIDOIDEAE

During the first decade of this century the Snowdrop has changed in popular consciousness from a humble little flower in a grandmother's garden, a motif on a million greetings cards, perhaps the focus of an early spring walk in a West Country valley white with the flowers – to a really expensive and desirable fashion object! Like the great 'tulipomania' craze of the seventeenth century, when fortunes were made and lost by collectors mad for the latest 'flame' or 'feather' marking the petals of Dutch tulips, Snowdrops have been swept up in a similar way. 'White Fever', as it is known in Holland, is causing extraordinary prices to be paid by collectors, and fans in England, Ireland, Scotland, Wales, Belgium, Germany and the Netherlands are all taking part in the frenzy. The dedicated fans are called 'Galanthophiles', and brave the worst of February weather to stand around comparing minute differences in green markings on the tiny flower bells. These green markings, along with the shape and size of the 'drop', are what distinguish the hundreds of named Snowdrop variants. Most distinguishing marks are on the 'inners' (think of variations on the usual green border edging the inner tube) but any green on the outer white 'petals' is also highly desirable.

Luckily for any of us who just want a pretty early spring garden, much of the craze is focused on other Snowdrop species, such as *Galanthus elwesii* and *G. plicatus* from the Crimea and western Turkey, which are larger and have many interesting variations in flower markings. *G. nivalis* has its own list of variants, from the very widespread double form to the rarities that have golden ovaries and markings instead of green, but it is always a more modest plant than the

LEFT: **Massed** *Galanthus nivalis* **in a Gloucestershire copse.** OPPOSITE PAGE: **Pretty garden grouping of Snowdrops and** *Cyclamen coum* **round a white-barked birch.**

continental species. It is entertaining on a sunny day to keep a look out among big patches of Snowdrops when the flowers open to show their green marks, and see if you can spot an oddity, a 'different' one. Our *G. nivalis* is found across much of Europe except in the continental west, and like several of our garden-worthy 'wild' flowers, this species is probably not a British native. It was known in Tudor gardens, Gerard (1597) grew it under the quaint name 'Timely flowring Bulbus violet' (timely meaning early, in good time), and gardeners may have adapted 'Snow-drop' a century or so later from German *Schnee-tropfen* or Swedish *Snödroppe*. An older English name may be 'Candlemas Bells', as Candlemas is the Feast of the Purification (2 February). White is of course associated with purity, and therefore with the Virgin Mary, and this may account for the frequent natural-ized populations of Snowdrops in churchyards and near religious settlements. It seems very possible, considering how important gardens were to monas-tic foundations, and how widely monks travelled in Europe for education and pilgrimage, that they intro-duced this plant (among many others) into Britain in medieval times. Professional horticulturalists in Tudor London obviously did not know it as a wild flower, but that does not mean that it could not have been

quietly becoming naturalized in the countryside. It is still extremely abundant in some areas, for instance Shropshire and the Welsh Marches.

'Wild' populations are usually found in dampish copses and woodland, and this well-known plant demonstrates perfectly the needs of a number of early-flowering bulbs, which can tolerate deep shade during summer when the bulb is safely packed up underground, but which must have spring light when the leaves are showing. Such bulbs are fine under deciduous trees, or in places where large-leaved perennials or ferns will dominate later, but their winter habitat must be as light as possible. Like-wise, they can be quite wet while they are in growth, but need to be drier when dormant, to prevent the bulbs rotting. The message is simple: winter and spring light, and good drainage, are the essentials. There are countless ways to enjoy Snowdrops even in the smallest garden, because they can be fitted under leafless branches of quite low-growing shrubs, be used in any tubs, pots or troughs which remain cool in the summer, be planted in drifts in short grass or under taller shrubs. They look good with primroses, with 'little blue bulbs', with miniature and species Daffodils and Cyclamen, and with Winter Aconites. Bressingham Gardens designed a classic planting of

Snowdrops with the so-called 'Black-grass' *Ophio-pogon planiscapus* 'Nigrescens' AGM, under the coral-coloured twigs of the small Dogwood *Cornus sanguinea* 'Midwinter Fire' – a perfect combination.

The perceived wisdom that Snowdrops must always be moved 'in the green' is arguable. Snowdrops are indeed only easy to find and dig up when the leaves are visible, and this seems to have led to the belief that it is actually good for them to be moved at this time. In fact, common sense should make it clear that moving bulbs in full growth, when the leaves and roots are working flat out to fill the bulb with food and energy for the dormant season and to start the next year, is probably not a good idea. Leaves get bruised, roots get torn, and the replanted bulb has lost its ability to collect and store food during a crucial part of its season when longer hours of sunlight are likely. Many gardeners have experienced the disappointment of a treasured new bulb which 'did nothing' in the second year, and transplant damage while in growth is probably the reason. Equally, *Galanthus nivalis* (and other species) bought as dry bulbs may have little life left in them, being too dried out. This sadly applies to most Snowdrops collected in the wild – the long collecting, packing and transport process, from Turkish hillside to Dutch bulb catalogue for instance, kills many of them. The very best way to get new Snowdrops is either to buy them in pots, and plant them out after the leaves have stopped work and gone yellow; to get a clump from a friend and replant them *very* carefully with as little disturbance as possible; or to order them from specialist nurserymen who will only send them to you at a suitable time.

Helleborus foetidus (Stinking Hellebore); *H. viridis* (Green Hellebore)

RANUNCULACEAE *(Buttercup family)*

The names of the two British hellebores are a source of irritation to people who admire them in the wild or grow and love them. The 'Stinking Hellebore' in particular seems unfairly labelled, because there is no 'stink' unless you crush the plant, and it is outstandingly handsome. 'Green Hellebore' just sounds dull and dim, the name giving little clue to the species' subtle beauty. They are both excellent garden plants, and *H. foetidus* in particular has a long season of interest. They are both considered to be native, and can be found on calcareous soils in the southern half of Britain (not north of the border or in Ireland), though both are uncommon. Hellebores were used in folk medicine throughout Europe – rather dangerously because they are all poisonous – and 'stinking' may refer to the unpleasant smell and taste of the potions produced. Gilbert White mentions such a dose being given to children infected with parasites, but says rather wryly, 'Where it killed not the patient… it would certainly kill the worms'. Another old name was 'Setterwort', coming from a veterinary use. Bizarrely, cattle with coughs or breathing problems had a 'seton' or thread made from a bit of hellebore root inserted into the windpipe to keep it clear.

Helleborus foetidus is unusual in its habit of growth. We are mostly familiar with the 'Lenten Roses' (hybrids of *H. orientalis* and other eastern European species) and the 'Christmas Rose' (*H. niger*), all of which have the flower stems budding from the centre of the plant, separate from the leaf stalks. They have semi-evergreen leaves which begin to die back during the winter – indeed *H. niger* usually has none when the flowers come up – and new leaves unfold after flowering. Green Hellebore has this growth pattern, but *H. foetidus* produces one sturdy stem with many evergreen leaves growing off it, and the flower cluster sprouting from the top. This is partly what gives it so many decorative months, because the dark leaves are sharply architectural all autumn, with the cluster of

RAINBOW WONDERS

Hellebores are basically buttercups, as their family name states, and in the wild they have simple open cup-shaped flowers with fine anthers to attract the attention of spring-flying insects. Many have green or yellowish flowers; others (mostly in the Balkans and further east) are sombre dark reds and purples. Before the middle of the last century choice for gardeners was limited. Breeding experiments had started, but only the now-familiar range of reddish-green 'Lenten Roses' was widely available, selections from *H. orientalis*. Recently, however, there has been a huge rush forward in breeding, hellebores are a big fashion and the variety of form and colour available is extraordinary. In this international frenzy, with new wonders emerging every year, our two native species have been rather lost, but still deserve a valued place in the garden.

New hybrid hellebores at Ashwood Nurseries near Kidderminster.

pale jade green buds visibly crowning the plant by Christmas. Flowers open during January and February, usually with each bell showing a thin crimson rim.

Even when the flowers are over they remain green into the early summer, and it is worth tolerating some of the 'untidy' phase in late summer when the spent

LEFT: Shapely plants of *H. foetidus* in a winter garden.
ABOVE: *H. foetidus* 'Wester Flisk' has reddish stems.

heads are brown to make sure that the plant has had a chance to seed. This species is not long-lived, and in garden conditions can 'seed itself to death', but seedlings are nice looking from the start, and can be moved to good places while they are young, so its self-seeding ability is usually welcome. Curiously, snails can be helpful with this remarkable plant. The only part which they eat is the fleshy seed capsule, which is fine because the seeds themselves are unpalatable, with an oily coat which sticks to the snail slime, so the snails move them round the garden where they germinate in suitable places. It is particularly useful because it is not fussy about position and can grow in open sun or in semi-shade, so long as the roots are cool and have some moisture. In the wild it can be seen on limestone scree and cliff ledges, as well as on banks and in open woodland. If you want to grow it from seed, stick to the rule for other hellebores – plant the seed fresh and *do not* try to pamper seedlings in a greenhouse or tunnel, but keep the seed tray outdoors in cool shade. Small plants make little fuss about moving, but don't try to shift flowering specimens. In the garden it can be grown in limey or neutral soils (but avoid peat), and if you can't acquire it from a local garden it should be available from a number of specialist nurseries, and it often

A wise choice! *H.foetidus* planted with Snowdrops and a form of the native Great Woodrush, *Luzula sylvatica* 'Aurea'.

turns up at local plant sales. Several selections are available, including the very attractive 'Wester Flisk' which has red stems. Be wary about putting new, commercially bought plants close to other hellebores unless they come from an expert grower and reliable source. Much-travelled plants can bring diseases with them – keep them 'in quarantine' for a season to see

Pure green tones, light veins and pretty anthers make the modest Green Hellebore a treasure.

light. The Green Hellebore's flower is a very pure colour, rather a jade green, with the veins drawing paler lines inside the cup. The prominent pollen anthers add to the beauty – in this species they are usually the colour of unsalted butter, but have occasionally been reported being darker or even purple. Unlike the evergreen *H. foetidus*, the leaves of this species die down 'for a rest' in the autumn, so are coming up fresh at flowering time, and the whole plant shows a pristine variety of greens. It has been quite overtaken by the dazzling modern hybrids, but can be very rewarding in green plantings, and is beautiful with early daffodils such as 'February Gold' or 'Peeping Tom', and of course the native *Narcissus pseudonarcissus* or its continental equivalent *N. lobularis*.

Hellebores in gardens often have a hard life, because they have acquired a reputation for needing deep shade, and this is quite wrong. Wild species, in England and on the continent, grow in light deciduous scrub, among scattered bushes on grassy banks and on stream sides. In Turkey one of the pure forms of *H. orientalis* can often be seen among limestone rocks under scattered tall trees, where plants are in full sun at flowering time. Semi-shade is the secret of making them happy, with as much light as possible available in the winter. In summer they do like to be cool, so leafy shade is fine then, but in year-round deep shade they will flower very poorly, and clumps will not bulk up. Once clumps of Green Hellebore are established they can be extremely long-lived, and are easily propagated by division, while Stinking Hellebore will re-seed itself. If Green Hellebore keeps any old leaves over winter, they can be cut back in January to make room for the new leaves to come in – this is done with garden varieties, making the flowers show up well. Some Stinking Hellebore plants may be rather short-lived perennials, but when they start to look really shabby after flowering they are probably going to die anyway, so pull them out and enjoy the elegant foliage of the young plants which will have been left behind. All hellebores like nutritious soils, and should be fed every year

how they get on in your garden. Stinking Hellebore looks good with so many other plants, and is excellent furniture for a garden at empty times. The great alpine nurseryman Walter Ingwersen (1951) considered it 'unjustly' named and calls it 'most decorative and extraordinarily lasting'.

The same plantsman also praised *H. viridis*, writing, 'Green flowers have a strange power of attraction for me', and this fascination is still shared by many gardeners. Hellebore flowers have a lovely simple bowl shape, with veins in the petals showing up in sun-

Hyacinthoides non-scripta
(Bluebell)

**LILIACEAE *(Lily family)*,
subfamily 5 – SCILLOIDEAE**

Britain's favourite flower

For much of its existence the Botanical Society of the British Isles (BSBI), founded in 1836 and Britain's premier botanical recording society, had a characteristic wild Bluebell as its logo (the brand is now identified by a more modern, abstract image). In the 2002 Plantlife survey which asked members to vote for the wild flower they felt should represent their home county, Bluebells had so many votes that they had to be moved to a singular category as the flower representing the whole of Britain. So it is clear that this plant has a flagship position in the flora. This honour is appropriate, because Britain and Ireland have nearly half the world population – the Bluebell is a

BSBI

LEFT: This Bluebell defined the logo of the BSBI for decades.
ABOVE: Bluebells in perfect habitat in managed woodland. Note the lack of undergrowth.

strictly Atlantic species, thriving in the damp airs of the west coasts of Europe, and these islands have proportionately more than anywhere else in the world. It is unknown in Scandinavia or further east than the

CONSERVATION – KILL OR CURE?

Ironically, the beginning of serious nature conservation, in the 1950s, for a time did as much harm to managed habitats as development did. There was a belief that 'nature' would make land go 'back to the wild' in a desirable way, and that wild creatures and plants would flourish. The fact that people and their domestic animals had influenced the whole countryside for centuries seemed to be ignored, so the short sheep-grazed grass of 'nature reserves' on the chalk downs became a tangle of thorn bushes rather than an open sward of Cowslips, while 'protected' woods became impenetrable thickets of brambles, ivy and weedy saplings. The 'lowest common denominator' was winning, and species richness decreased. It has only recently been widely recognized that traditional management needs to be acknowledged and applied as an essential conservation tool. Two particular types of woodland, 'lowland Beech and Yew' and 'lowland mixed deciduous', which are both good for Bluebells, are considered threatened enough to have been given 'UK BAPs' (Biodiversity Action Plans) under European law, to try to save them, and the restoration of traditional management has to be part of this effort.

Pure wild Bluebells – deep blue narrow bells on a curving stem.

nearest parts of Germany, and is really limited to Britain and Ireland, parts of Belgium and the Netherlands, and France. *Hyacinthoides non-scripta* also grows in the cooler areas of Spain and Portugal, where it meets the natural distribution of a close relative *H. hispanica* (the Spanish Bluebell), and by a quirk of garden history this cousin has become a threat to our native species.

Primrose lanes, Heather moors and Bluebell woods are part of what makes the popular image of Britain – pictures and references must outnumber even Beefeaters, the White Cliffs of Dover or the London Eye, and most people would be horrified to know that Bluebell woods in particular are in real danger. Bluebells have thrived for many centuries with the way that our woods have been managed, because regular cycles of tree felling (such as those still maintained in the fence-pole Sweet Chestnut coppices of the Kent and Sussex Weald) allows light into the understorey for a few years. Plants of the woodland floor mostly need winter and spring light, before they die back during the shady summer, and wood management, like natural tree falls, allows them periodic rations of this precious commodity to strengthen their growth. In modern life though, management is becoming rare. Most timber comes from plantation conifers, home-grown or imported, because they grow fast and cheaply, and there are fewer landowners every year who can employ skilled foresters. Bluebells grow in deciduous woods, under broadleaved trees such as Beech, Ash and Hornbeam, and so much of this kind of woodland has been destroyed, or is now unmanaged and choked with ivy and brambles, that the habitat and all its plants are considered under threat.

The poor Bluebell is, and has been for more than half a century, endangered by both habitat destruction and mismanagement, and it is now thought to have a more insidious threat – hybridization. The Spanish Bluebell has been in gardens in Britain and Ireland since the seventeenth century. It grows easily (and is difficult to eradicate), and the pretty pale blue, pink or white flowers are familiar in the suite of plants labelled 'cottage garden'. It is often present on road banks, and in patches of scrub where there were once buildings, orchards or gardens. Even more frequently a very similar plant will be found, looking like the Spanish Bluebell, but it is actually the Garden Bluebell, *Hyacinthoides × massartiana*, the hybrid between the wild native *H. non-scripta* and the garden foreigner *H. hispanica*. Now that Britain is so crowded, with roads and railway lines linking habitats, wild and garden plants meet more often and at closer quarters than before, and the hybrid bluebell seems to be becoming more common and has been found edging into native populations. The invader has hybrid vigour, and in some places seems to be taking over valuable growing space from its wild cousin.

So our top British wild flower is actually in a lot of trouble, though this can be hard to believe when there is a sea of blue right through a wood or on a bracken hillside, and its story chimes with what has happened, or is still happening, to a number of our precious native plants. One type of misfortune may concern the introduction of a foreign plant, such as Giant Hogweed or Japanese Knotweed, which adapts easily to our climate and invades native habitats. In this case the incomer is also a close relative, the

Hybrid Bluebells have soft blue, open 'bells' with pale anthers, on an upright stem.

species are compatible, and bees do buzz around spring pollen, so tough and vigorous hybrids are occurring too often. There is also a paradoxical element in conservation – a plant can be too common for its own good. Plant conservation has always been underfunded and it is useless trying to raise funds when those with money can say 'but I see that all over the place', so it is almost impossible to save a species from decline until it is in real danger, and the Bluebell has only hitched a lift towards legal protection by being part of two threatened woodland habitats.

The only safeguard which it has had for more than a decade is a law forbidding the digging up of wild bulbs to sell, except with a licence, which is quite hard to obtain. This has done some good, but it does make life more difficult for ethical gardeners who want to grow the true Bluebell. 'English' or 'wild' stock is frequently advertised, but it is often hard to discover what this actually means, and many of the bulbs will have been imported, or turn out to be the hybrid anyway. The best thing, as with many other wild flowers, is to make friends with someone who has them growing abundantly, and be given some bulbs. They increase quite rapidly, and like to be in their own company – they will crowd out other spring species grown with them. If you have Spanish or Garden Bluebells already in your garden or close by (bees forage for several miles) you will be able to observe the interesting slide into hybridization, but it may be hard to keep pure plants in the long run. All in all, beautiful as they are, it is probably best to campaign to try to save them where they are growing already, rather than put time and energy into getting them into your garden. Spanish and Garden Bluebells are easy and cheerful spring bulbs, excellent cut flowers, and only a problem if you want to clear them away if you are afraid of them 'infecting' a nearby bluebell wood.

The hybrids are variable, and it can be hard to distinguish Garden Bluebell from Spanish forms, but the native Bluebell is unmistakable. The bells are a strong blue ('white Bluebells' are a rare find in native populations), elegantly narrow, hanging along one side of the gracefully curved spike.

Garden and Spanish Bluebells are frequently white or pink, or varying shades of pale chalky blue. The 'bells' are wide open, and don't really hang down, but look directly outwards round most of the straight sturdy spike. The native Bluebell has narrow leaves (7–15mm wide) while the others are wider (10–35mm), though leaf characters can be confusing unless you have some of each kind to compare. One of the most useful differences can be the colour of the anthers, which are blue and almost hidden in the bells of the native, but usually cream-coloured (at least when fully mature) and clearly visible in Spanish Bluebell and most hybrids.

Leucojum aestivum (Summer Snowflake, Loddon Lily)

LILIACEAE (Lily family), subfamily 7 – AMARYLLIDOIDEAE

County flower of Berkshire

This is the most rewarding of wild bulbs to grow in the garden. It is easy to establish, flowers reliably for at least two months, has no invasive habits, and is very long-lived. It is also very beautiful. William Robinson, in his influential book The Wild Garden (1870) noted its value for 'wild grassy places', and remembering a visit to Longleat wrote, 'I have rarely seen anything more beautiful than a colony of the Summer Snowflake' beside a group of shrubs. The great nurseryman Walter Ingwersen (1951) commented on how 'the clumps increase in beauty from year to year', while Robert Gathorne-Hardy (1961) called it 'the loveliest of natives'. In the wild it is usually found in an unlikely-looking habitat, which John Grigson described with a nice touch of drama in The Englishman's Flora (1958):

Imagine, if you have never seen the wild Loddon Lily, a black swamp on the edge of the Thames, alders or willows overhead, a swamp which quivers and soggs and stinks. In the gloom... white flowers hanging in a severe purity from the end of long stems.

Leucojum aestivum **ssp.** *aestivum* **on the River Barrow in Ireland. The wide green-tipped bells grow four or five to a stem above strong clumps of leaves.**

Wild populations are best known from the Thames and its tributaries, in particular the Lodden, from the Stour in Dorset, and in Ireland from large southern rivers such as the Barrow, the Slaney and the Suir. The habitat is generally as Grigson described, in wet hollows by the river bank, and sometimes on small willow-covered islets, which are under water for most of the winter, sludged with almost bare mud when spring lowers the water level a bit, and in summer becoming a tangle of nettles. The depressing sight of plastic bags caught in drooping willow branches at high water mark could actually lead to a good place to find the flower! This strange home means that it can tolerate really wet conditions in winter, and it is ideal for making something of nasty damp corners in the garden. Although it does not want to be right in water while growing and flowering, it will tolerate winter flooding and permanent dampness, and will compete successfully with grass (it occasionally grows in damp meadows). In the garden it will tolerate much drier conditions, but does appreciate good and reasonably moisture-retentive soils. The unat-

tractive wild habitats do provide plenty of nutrition, because of silt deposited by winter floods. The Loddon Lily is similar to many of our spring flowers (and many commonly grown continental bulbs) in needing winter and spring light, and will only grow in the open or under deciduous shade.

Like two of our other favourite spring bulbs, Fritillary and Snowdrop, its history is rather mysterious. It grows at least a foot tall, in large clumps, and sometimes in spectacular quantity, so is not easily overlooked, but its first record in the wild was not made until 1780, when the botanist William Curtis found it by the Thames 'between Greenwich and Woolwich'. He questioned its origin himself, asking 'how so ornamental a plant, growing in so public a place, could have escaped... prying eyes... for such a length of time'. He and others have suggested that it must be a garden escape, but it can be found in identical flood-plain habitats to ours throughout Europe, and there are still two strong schools of thought – botanists have never agreed on whether it is native or introduced.

Typical wild
Daffodil flowers
with narrow gold
trumpets and
slightly twisting
pale petals.

There are no academic disagreements though about its value in the garden, and it is widely available from bulb merchants, so there are no tricky ethical questions about obtaining it. If you want to be picky, it is worth noting that there are two forms known in gardens. The real wild plant is *Leucojum aestivum* ssp. *aestivum*, which has fairly wide flower bells, and the edges of its three-cornered stem are smooth unless you feel very carefully at the bottom. *L. aestivum* ssp. *pulchellum* has rather smaller, narrow bells, and the angles of the stems feel rough from top to bottom if you run a finger down. This is the old 'cottage garden' variety, and the long-lived clumps are often found as a relic of former gardens. Both grow equally well. The 'Summer Snowflake' name is really only to distinguish this plant from another species, *Leucojum vernum* (Spring Snowflake), which is widely distributed as a wild plant on the continent and usually flowers first, but the first flowers of the Loddon Lily are usually out in February or early March, and will go on being produced till May if it is not too hot. Leaves will die down to rest during summer and autumn. There is an excellent garden selection which is widely available, 'Gravetye Giant', named after William Robinson's house Gravetye Manor.

Narcissus pseudonarcissus (Daffodil, Lent Lily)

LILIACEAE *(Lily family)*, subfamily 7 – AMARYLLIDOIDEAE

County flower of Gloucestershire

If you are interested in the wild plants of Britain, in their histories and their relationship with us, there is no better book to own than Richard Mabey's *Flora Britannica* (1996), and his account of the Daffodil goes way beyond the story of William Wordsworth and his sister Dorothy wandering 'lonely as a cloud' by Coniston Water in the Lake District (where the Daffodils still grow), and is filled with marvellous stories. To grow this species in the garden though takes very little specialist information. Formerly one of the most widespread and abundant flowers in England and Wales (though not Ireland or Scotland) it is now more scattered, but still very well-known and beloved in Devon for instance; along the Welsh Marches (particularly parts of Gloucestershire and Herefordshire); near Ferndale in Yorkshire; in the Lake District and the Sussex Weald. Local pride (and local tourist businesses!) usually keep this iconic plant from being threatened by development.

Daffodils in low spring sunlight in a garden. Shade in summer will not matter.

If you grow any other daffodil in your garden, you will be able to grow the native. It is generally less fussy than some of the continental species of *Narcissus*, and because it was once common throughout England and Wales there are no worries about its reaction to climate variations throughout. It can of course also be grown in Ireland and Scotland. In general it probably likes to be left fairly undisturbed, in places resembling a woodland edge or clearing, or in open grassland. The 'rules' for native spring flowers in gardens are the same for most: encourage as much light as possible in winter and early spring: plant where there is little competition at flowering time: don't mow grassland plants till they have quite died down, but at some point in the year pretend to be a sheep, cow or hay cutter and clear away any thuggish grasses. The Lent Lily, so named for its flowering time, also appreciates not getting too dry or hot in summer. It can be planted in autumn like any dry bulb. Probably the most difficult part of getting it into your garden is finding the pure species.

There are a number of small daffodils around with the familiar pale outer petals and gold trumpets, but exactly what they are is often a puzzle even to experts. Daffodils have been popular garden plants for more than 500 years, and continental wild species as well as garden selections have been imported throughout that time. Variation and hybridization has

ANCIENT AND MODERN

In recent years a well-meaning habit has grown up of individuals and local councils 'decorating' road verges with plantings of large modern daffodil cultivars. Within town and village boundaries this is accepted and enjoyed, but out in the countryside it has become controversial. The plants look out of place, and exclude native species – even the Welsh Government has said that the country has 'too many daffodils'. However, hedge banks, field borders, road verges and copses near former estates may have much more historic plants naturalized over many years, such as the ancient golden double 'Van Sion', its trumpet tightly packed with frilly partial petals, sometimes splitting to show a ragged bunch; various 'old-fashioned narcissus' varieties with small cups and soft yellow, orange or whitish colours; and the charming fragrant *N. × medioluteus* (sometimes called 'Primrose-peerless'), which has two or three flowers on a stem and is a hybrid between *N. tazetta*, the highly scented parent of the famous 'Soleil d'Or', and the Pheasant's-eye *N. poeticus*. In former daffodil-growing areas such as the Tamar Valley in Cornwall later escapes, cultivars bred in the 1940s and '50s, are often seen in the hedges, relics of an earlier trade when millions of cut flowers were grown and sent to London by train. Our wild Daffodil is iconic, but it is not the only member of the *Narcissus* genus to be closely woven into both our garden and economic histories, and into art and literature.

occurred both in the wild and in gardens, and bulbs now available in the horticultural trade may have acquired several different names, sometimes none of which are botanically correct. *Narcissus 'lobularis'* is a good example – it can be found on many bulb lists, but may not be a correct name for anything by now! Unless you very particularly want to be sure that

Star-of-Bethlehem flowers open in spring sunlight. The name is derived from their shape.

you have the English wild species, there are several alternative small bicolour trumpet daffodils which give much the same effect in plantings. Many of the 'lobularis' variants will do the job well, as will almost anything listed as *N. pseudonarcissus*. You may be lucky enough to have or get the real thing, but aesthetically a number of varieties will give a similarly magical effect.

There is another daffodil that may be native, though botanists have argued about this. *Narcissus obovallaris*, the Tenby Daffodil, is an oddity because it is not known as a wild plant anywhere else in the world. Southwest Wales was a busy place in ancient times, well settled and quite wealthy, so there will have been gardens, and the most likely origin for this excellent form is that it was an early garden sport. Once abundant in that part of Wales, it was 'discovered' and dug up for the demands of the horticultural trade in the nineteenth century, nearly obliterating any extensive wild-looking populations. It has since been somewhat restored by planting, and it is perfectly distinct — a delightfully chubby little all-gold daffodil, weather-proof and early. Bulbs bought from lists should be exactly what they say, as it is now widely commercially grown, and it is very good indeed naturalized in open grass.

Ornithogalum angustifolium, syn.* O. umbellatum ssp. campestre (Star-of-Bethlehem); O. pyrenaicum (Spiked Star-of-Bethlehem, Bath Asparagus)

LILIACEAE *(Lily family)*, subfamily 5 – SCILLOIDEAE

There are about thirty-five of the *Ornithogalum* genus found across Europe, and more in Asia. Many of them are pretty and garden-worthy, and may be familiar from bulb lists and garden literature, but only two have just a toe-hold as British natives. They are both modest in appearance and uncommon in the wild, but we have few native bulbs, and they are pleasant and well-behaved enough to be welcome denizens in the spring garden. A third species, *O. nutans* (Drooping Star-of-Bethlehem), is sometimes found naturalized, and may be described as a wild flower, but it is not native. It is widely available, and its green-and-white bells can look lovely with new fern growth or Wood Anemones in semi-shade.

The dainty flowers of Wood-sorrel in mossy shade.

O. angustifolium may be sold, or mentioned in gardening and wild flower books, as *O. umbellatum*. This was considered to be a very similar species, found in Europe, and the names and identities have been variously used and changed, as is shown in the latest version given above. Whatever the name, this little star grows well in sunlight, in short grass or troughs, beds or rockeries. It likes sandy soil.

O. pyrenaicum is rather a plain plant of woods and shady hedge banks in central England. It is always something of a rarity, but has gathered a great deal of interest and speculation over the years. As one of its common names, Bath Asparagus, suggests, it is particularly associated with the environs of the city, and is sometimes said to have been brought there by the Romans, on purpose to grow as a vegetable, or by chance with roots of the vines which they grew there. The 'vegetable' is the flower spikes, cut and eaten in bud in the same way as garden asparagus. When the 'nouvelle cuisine' fashion arrived in the 1980s there was a rush of interest in this rare wild food, and conservationists feared that it would be endangered by suddenly regaining a commercial value. Its use became controversial, and still is, because any harvesting of such a scarce plant, combined with all the other threats in modern life, must be irresponsible. Bath residents are usually loyal, watching over their local populations. If you want to try it, grow it! The tallish stems (up to 100cm) are leafless, and topped with a crowded spike of about twenty flowers. The shape is good and upstanding, but the flower colour is frankly rather dull, a greeny-yellow which needs careful placing to stand out in the garden, and leaves have died down before flowering. It prefers calcareous soils, and does well in semi-shade.

Oxalis acetosella (Wood-sorrel)

OXALIDACEAE *(Wood-sorrel family)*

Gardeners who have struggled with any of the pesky foreign *Oxalis* species which have become established in our gardens as extremely invasive weeds, may be horrified to see the native Wood-sorrel recommended as a garden plant. However, this dainty species is difficult in a completely opposite sense as it is none too easy to persuade it to establish. Its habitat in the wild is in woodland and on rocks, among tree roots on hedge or river banks, generally where the atmosphere remains humid all year round. Typically it grows on or among mosses. William Robinson (1870) recommended it for the wild garden, calling it 'a chaste little plant'. He mentions its natural habitat

Herb-Paris in flower. Plants may have five leaves rather than the usual four.

being 'woody places... and over mossy stumps' so it should be put in the garden 'where there is a little diversity of surface, or half shady spots'. It is perfect for a stumpery (however small). The trefoil leaves (imagine a bright green shamrock leaf nearly an inch across) can be held spread, but at night or in very dark weather they will fold down like umbrella spokes. The little white flowers, usually with pinkish veins, are held above the leaves on threadlike stalks. If you have a part of the garden with mossy tree roots, or a shady damp rockery or stream side, it is worth trying to establish this exquisite little plant. Sometimes it will settle under shelves or staging on the shady side of a shed where it is always fairly cool and damp, but it does take care and attention to get it going, checking that it never dries right out when planted. In many of its natural habitats it grows on pure leaf mould, and possibly only a very thin layer of this, so rich garden soil is not what is needed.

The name 'Wood-sorrel' comes from the taste of the leaves, which have the same sharpness as Sorrel itself (*Rumex acetosa*). The older names include 'Cuckoo's Bread-and-Cheese', and there can hardly be anyone brought up in the countryside who has not picked a leaf or two to chew (or indeed added it to sandwiches), but now the days of Health and Safety have come, Wood-sorrel is not considered an acceptable food. Eaten in quantity it can be somewhat toxic – but the labour involved in picking even one helping of the

thin leaves, and the probable nastiness of the result if cooked, make harmful events extremely unlikely!

Paris quadrifolia (Herb-Paris)

LILIACEAE *(Lily family)*, subfamily 4 – LILIOIDEAE

This extraordinary-looking woodlander is present throughout much of central Britain, but not in the western or northern extremities or in Ireland. It is not classed as nationally rare, but is never a common plant, and its looks and life-style make it difficult to spot, so it is little known. It grows in leaf-litter in woods on calcareous soils, and is nearly always found among a mixture of other plants such as *Mercurialis perennis* (Dog's Mercury), Bluebells, Wood Anemones or *Lamiastrum galeobdolon* (Yellow Archangel, whose closely related variegated subspecies *L. galeobdolon* ssp. *argentatum* infests many an old shrubbery). As the photograph shows, in spite of the very distinctive whorl of leaves on the stem of Herb-Paris, the flowers are odd and inconspicuous, making plants hard to pick out from the surrounding greenery, though of course this makes it a thrilling flower to find if you are successful. It's actually easier to appreciate its looks when it is grown in gardens

Solomon's-seal growing in worked hazel coppice, where cutting cycles allow light to reach the understorey.

where it may be less lost to view in a mass of green. Christopher Lloyd liked it, saying that although it is 'demure in colouring' the interesting shape of the plant and its ability to form nice colonies 'is always arresting' (2000). Members of the *Paris* genus have attracted gardeners for a long time. The better-known and much more spectacular *P. polyphylla* was introduced from the Himalayas in 1826, and was enough in general circulation to get an admiring mention in Graham Stuart Thomas' popular *Perennial Garden Plants*, which came out in 1976, though he admitted that it was a rarity.

The 'Paris' in the name is nothing to do with the French capital, or with the rash young demi-god of Greek mythology who was instrumental in the start of the Trojan Wars. It is much more mundane, coming from apothecaries' Latin *herba paris*, meaning 'pair herb'. All its parts, leaves, stamens, styles, ovary compartments, are usually in matched pairs – twice two of each – and it was sometimes called the 'herb of equality'. The leaves sometimes break this rule, producing six (or an uneven five), but it can be hard to tell whether the blades are really separate, or have split as they opened out.

If you live on chalk or limestone, and part of your garden is shady and rich in leaf mould, and if you

admire beauty in curious forms, this is a very appealing plant to try. It is not widely available, but specialist nurseries with an interesting range of woodland plants might well grow it. Once seen it cannot be forgotten. Christopher Lloyd referred to the flower of another *Paris* species as 'this artifact' and the bizarre but graceful flower, its only colours black, green and primrose, do seem like a fantasy structure. If you can get plants, settle them in a hopeful spot and leave them be – they do not like being moved around.

Polygonatum multiflorum (Solomon's-seal)

LILIACEAE *(Lily family)*, subfamily 4 – LILIOIDEAE

There are actually four Solomon's-seals scattered in Britain. The best-known, *P. multiflorum* (Solomon's-seal), is fairly widespread in woods and shady hedgerows in central and southern Britain. Two, *P. odoratum* (Angular Solomon's-seal) and *P. verticillatum* (Whorled Solomon's-seal) are extremely rare and outside the scope of this book. The fourth, *P. ×*

Primroses are close to our hearts, as shown in the quarry-men's graveyard on Portland, Dorset.

hybridum (Garden Solomon's-seal) is the most commonly grown. It originated as a hybrid between *P. multiflorum* and *P. odoratum*, and is often found as a naturalized escape. It looks very like *P. multiflorum*, and for garden appearance either can be used. They are most handsome plants with their beautifully arched stems hung with groups of small pale bells, and are tall enough to be grown for height behind other spring plantings. They prefer calcareous soils with some leaf-mould, and thrive in semi-shade, or even deep shade if the canopy does not close to dark until June.

Solomon's-seal has one enemy in the garden. The Solomon's-seal sawfly (*Phymatocera aterrima*) has larvae that hatch in spring, producing caterpillars which can completely strip the plants. In some years they do not appear until well into June; in others they seem earlier and can damage plants still in flower. Like most sawfly grubs, these caterpillars are pretty unattractive, and the only effective way of dealing with them is to pick them off. Bird-table birds may or may not accept them, so sometimes they have to be squashed and composted. Don't let this put you off growing this wonderfully decorative plant – the grubs won't turn up until you have had time to enjoy its beauty, and if you keep an eye out for the first hatch, you can

protect the leaves for quite a while. After all, sawflies have to live too, and this one is completely limited to this plant and can eat nothing else.

The origin of the quaint name is too archaic to be obvious now, as it is thought that the dangling flowers were compared to the dangling seals attached to medieval documents. The actual Seal of Solomon was the pentangle, the five-pointed star symbolizing the five wounds of Christ, but this has no visible link to the plant.

Primula elatior (Oxlip); *P. veris* (Cowslip); *P. vulgaris* (Primrose)

PRIMULACEAE *(Primrose family)*

County flower of Suffolk: Oxlip; Northamptonshire, Surrey and Worcestershire: Cowslip; Devon: Primrose

It would be hard to imagine modern towns and gardens without primroses and polyanthus. With the 'winter pansy' they give colour to streets, parks and roundabouts throughout the cold months, and are

ABOVE: **Primroses and Cowslips hybridized to give the ancestor of our polyanthus.**
RIGHT: **Flying the colours! Wild** P. *vulgaris* **ssp.** *sibthorpii* **near Istanbul.**

cherished in window boxes and door-step containers. These flowers are very much larger and more brightly coloured than their wild relatives, and are produced by breeders as a significant part of the horticultural trade, but curiously the position of all of them in the national consciousness has been similar for hundreds of years. The word 'iconic' can be over-used when it comes to our wild flowers – so many are really important for their place in art, literature, and national and local pride – but it really defines the position of Primroses and Cowslips (the Oxlip is less familiar). From medieval 'millefleurs' tapestries, to Pre-Raphaelite pictures, to the trillions of cards, fabrics, tea towels and containers that feature them today, they are instantly recognizable even to people who have never been lucky enough to see them in the countryside.

The Primrose itself is the commonest species, and Primroses have several characteristics that contribute to their perfection as spring garden plants. They grow naturally in sun or dappled shade, on banks and roadsides, in managed woodland, in cliff grassland and among bracken, on stream sides, and they have simple needs, principally a soil that will not dry out too much, or get too hot. Their lifestyle is adjusted to respond to our winter and spring weather: the leaves begin to appear in tight little bunches before Christ-

mas, making ready to expand quickly when the temperature goes up; flowers start at the same signal, opening a bit faster than the leaves so they are visible to the first flying insects; both are in full growth in April (in the south), but by May surrounding vegetation has begun to overtop the early flowers, and Primroses now die back to spend the summer largely dormant in the cool shade of taller plants. This makes them ideal for the spring garden, because they can be planted underneath small shrubs or large border perennials where they will discreetly fade out after flowering. Of course they are also delightful in a wild garden or shrubbery, on the shady side of a rock garden, or allowed to self-seed along path edges or round fruit trees. Another trait which has been important throughout their garden history is their promiscuity. Primroses, Cowslips and Oxlips all easily produce hybrids, and the most frequent of these, the False Oxlip P. × *polyantha* (P. *vulgaris* × P. *veris*), is of course an important ancestor of the familiar 'polyanthus'.

Colour has also been important in the development of garden Primroses. Our wild plant occasionally throws colour variations, and as odd varieties were collectors' items in Tudor gardens (they were particularly keen on double flowers also, and strange

The graceful true Oxlip is rare now, but has been important in breeding.

'Jack-in-the-green' or 'Hose-in-hose' forms) these genes have been wandering back into the countryside for many years. Other species of *Primula* can also get mixed into garden-bred plants, so reds and purples were not uncommon early on. The Eastern European version of our common Primrose, *P. vulgaris* subsp. *sibthorpii*, is found in many shades of pink and purple. Given that modern plant breeding uses magical techniques to mix and match genetic material, it is not surprising that there is such an astonishing range of colour now available. However, some of these new plants are definitely 'in your face', and some gardeners prefer to stay with the venerable 'old Primrose' varieties in more muted tones. These can become a serious collector's passion, but the plants are often weak and difficult to grow, and are always rare, so the common pale yellow single-flowered Primrose is always the most practical choice.

Cowslips and Oxlips are less universally easy in the garden because they both need calcareous soils. Cowslips are happiest in short, sunny grassland, and are now usually seen on sheep-grazed chalk or limestone slopes where the land has been too steep to plough, though they have appeared in quantity on some main road and motorway verges on suitable soils. These areas have to be regularly mown, and the mowings removed to avoid risk of fire, and this man-

agement creates much the same conditions as grazing animals do. Oxlips are now very rare, restricted to a few boulder-clay woods in East Anglia. This true species is distinct from the hybrid False Oxlip in always having the flowers drooping, held rather gracefully to one side of the head.

It is available from specialist nurseries, and can be grown in rather damp limey soils, in semi-shade, making a lovely addition to a fern bed or shrubbery. Cowslips are altogether more casual about their situation, so long as they have sun and lime, and will self-seed. They can be allowed into paths, or along the edges of borders, and most delightfully added to lawns. They can also, like Primroses, be allowed into kitchen gardens. Children's books of the last century still sometimes mentioned making 'Cowslip balls' (sometimes called 'tosties': flower heads were tied together to make soft balls which could be rolled down slopes or thrown in games), and of course there was Cowslip wine; while these things are sadly impossible now, it can be a real joy to have enough self-seeded in your garden to pick guilt-free posies at least!

Cowslips have featured in an ethical question concerning the use of wild flowers in gardens, and in corporate 'restoration' projects. The most readily available seed often comes from continental sources, and from plants that have genetic differences from our natives. Many council-sown road verges have been planted with 'foreign' varieties of common plants (including Knapweed, Bird's-foot-trefoil and Cowslips), and many of the 'wild' plants sold at garden centres are the same. This concerns conservation workers, because these foreign strains will mix with our natives, and may introduce different behaviours and problems (like any foreign introduction). If you want to grow native plants, it is worth trying to find the real thing. Native Cowslips are nearly always a rich yellow (a red Cowslip used to be a real find), the bell-like flowers with quite narrow mouths, and usually hanging down; but continental varieties often show a whole range of colours, and the heads are often quite loosely arranged with wider-mouthed, more polyanthus-like flowers. These plants may also grow surprisingly large. They are fine in a flower bed, but

Narrow-leaved Lungwort has spotted leaves and intense blue flowers.

should not be established in any grassland where they might cross-breed with native plants. Getting seed or plants from specialist suppliers, who can tell you about the origin, is always possible.

Pulmonaria longifolia (Narrow-leaved Lungwort)

BORAGINACEAE (Borage family)

Although this gorgeous flower is very rare in the wild, it is possible to find some beautiful substitutes among the many *Pulmonaria* cultivars now available. Occasionally found on wood edges and partly shaded grassy verges in Dorset, the Isle of Wight and the New Forest, in the garden many of its relatives grow very well, given leaf mould and protected from exposure or any hot, dry conditions. The 2011 *Plant Finder* lists *P. longifolia* itself, the continental variant *P. longifolia* ssp. *cevennensis*, and six named garden selections, so it should be possible to find plants with the distinguishing features of the native species: narrow, dark green leaves with whitish spots, and flowers of a particularly intense strong blue. The familiar plant of old-fashioned gardens (*P. officinalis*), sometimes called 'Soldiers and Sailors' because of its pink or red buds opening to a soft blue, is a much less clear-cut and stylish plant, and the leaf-shape is more amorphous.

Pulmonaria species were formerly used in medicine, because the medieval belief in the 'doctrine of signatures' dictated that if a plant looked like a part of the body, it must be good for that part. The spotted leaves of lungworts were supposed to look like the texture of those organs. The specific name *'officinalis'* reveals that a plant has a medical history. When Carl Linnaeus was setting up the 'binomial' system in the

eighteenth century, putting each plant in a genus (e.g. *Pulmonaria*) and giving it a specific name of its own (e.g. *longifolia*), the '*officinalis*' tag was given to plants with a record of use by doctors and herbalists, the equivalent of the drug lists in the British Pharmacopoeia today.

Ranunculus ficaria, syn.* *Ficaria verna* (Lesser Celandine); *Ranunculus* spp. (Buttercups)

RANUNCULACEAE *(Buttercup family)*

This is one of the wild flowers that has a very bad reputation with gardeners, some of whom spend years trying to get rid of it, and nurserymen who sell any of the named selections are all too familiar with the shocked and scornful cries of potential customers! A blanket hostile reaction is not necessary though, and this very familiar little plant has some genuinely good qualities. Starting from basics, its appearance is delightful. When early sunny days in March (or even February in the south) open the cups of the first Celandines, revealing that incomparable gleam of gold inside the petals, it is the moment when spring arrives. It's an irresistible sight for country dwellers, and must feature in countless childhood memories, because when the flowers are closed in dark weather they are camouflaged in patterned greens and browns, almost invisible, so the opening is always a surprise. Like many of our spring flowers, Celandines produce their leaves after Christmas, flower mostly through March and April, and have died back and completely vanished by the middle of May. Their bad quality in relation to gardens is their efficiency — bad weather means nothing to them, the brilliant shine of the open petals attracts and guides every possible

OPPOSITE: **Buttercups on a Wiltshire common.**
ABOVE: **Celandines on a Somerset farm.**
LEFT: **The boldest of Celandines – 'Brazen Hussy'.**

pollinating insect, and as well as seeds they produce masses of little tubers all of which (however minute) can make a new plant. One form even produces extra tubers in its leaf axils, scattering these as well as its seeds when the plant dries up in May. Celandines grow almost anywhere, particularly in woods, on shady banks and stream sides, and in grassland which has been disturbed by ploughing or heavy grazing giving the plant a chance to spread. Spectacular displays sometimes appear on building sites, or on ground that has been cleared by weed-killers, but obviously this is the last thing which is wanted in a garden.

There are ways to enjoy the charming aspects, however, without spending years furiously trying to sieve tiny tubers out of your soil. For the last twenty years or so 'different' Celandines have been quite in fashion, with keen fans collecting the unusual colours and shapes that are sometimes found among ordinary wild plants. A few forms have been known and appre-

ciated for much longer. The admirable plantsman and garden writer E.A. Bowles, in *My Garden in Spring* (1914) acknowledges 'the common wild forms one constantly struggles with but cannot entirely expel', but praises the double forms (*R. ficaria* 'Flore Pleno' group) and a white single 'with a charming creamy tint ... as beautifully varnished as any Buttercup'. He also liked a large form, wild in Mediterranean countries, *R. ficaria* ssp. *chrysocephalus*, 'quite three times as large as the undesirable native'. Christopher Lloyd was also very fond of the double, praising its 'very tight rosette of yellow, green in the middle' (2000), and it was he who first found the now famous 'Brazen Hussy', which has gleaming mahogany leaves, and 'introduced [it] to civilized society'.

There are now over seventy named varieties listed in the *Plant Finder*, and many of them are very pretty (though 'Double Mud' may be an acquired taste), but most of them are unlikely to take over your garden, and some are quite difficult to keep going at all. In the

ABOVE: **Meadow Buttercup has 'Crowfoot'-shaped leaves.**
LEFT: **Bulbous Buttercup is shorter and stockier, always distinguishable by its folded-down sepals.**

DO YOU LIKE BUTTER?

It used to be easy (and occasionally still is) to find a handful of Buttercup flowers to hold under a friend's chin – the gold reflected onto their skin from the flowers always answers 'yes' to the old question. The three commonest native buttercups are *Ranunculus acris* (Meadow Buttercup or meadow Crowfoot), *R. bulbosus* (Bulbous Buttercup), and *R. repens* (Creeping Buttercup); these are the species which can sometimes turn grasslands quite gold.

Meadow Buttercup is the tallest, and used to be a characteristic flower of hay and water meadows before intensive farming made these grasslands less diverse. Bulbous Buttercup prefers calcareous soils, and can be seen on limestone and chalk grasslands, and on 'fixed' sand dunes which have become well vegetated. Creeping Buttercup is the weediest of the three, and likes damp habitat, so can be seen along roadside ditches and in muddy gateways, and can be a tough and annoying garden weed. All three have their admirers though,

because they can occasionally produce special flower shapes, and quite a range of colours in flower, leaf and stem. Both Meadow and Bulbous Buttercups can be double, and both have lovely pale forms, *R. acris* 'Citrinus' and *R. bulbosus* 'F.M. Burton'. Creeping Buttercup may be seen with red or purple colouring on stems or leaves, and some brave gardeners appreciate these variants enough to collect them to grow as specimen plants, but this species never loses its invasive habits. In fact none of these three buttercups, beautiful as they are, can really be recommended as a garden plant. *R. bulbosus* dies down in July, not coming into leaf again till the autumn, so it is really only practical to use it in a lawn or grass plot, and both it and *R. acris* can prove to be quite fussy about soil conditions, in particular regarding the timing and amount of available moisture. It is well worth trying to establish *R. acris* 'Citrinus' as a border, wild garden or pond edge plant, for its prettiness and long flowering season, but this common species can be unexpectedly difficult away from its usual habitat and plant community.

LEFT: **Selected double forms of Red Campion are really glamorous.**
ABOVE: **A pink form of wild Sea Campion on an Irish shingle beach.**

same way that variegated sports are often weaker than a plain green plant, the variant Celandines rarely multiply too vigorously. Doubles are unlikely to seed anyway, so if you leave the tubers undisturbed they will stay in one place. The 'giant' Mediterranean Celandine is a lovely plant, with quite bright green leaves and wonderful big flowers, but it usually has all too few seedlings, and if you were to experience an unexpected population explosion, all its parts are recognizably large from the first so seedlings could easily be captured. If the word 'Celandine' still makes you nervous of planting them out, they do make very pretty container plants. They need a wide pot of their own (a fairly shallow clay pan is attractive) which can be put away in a shady corner once they have died down. Plants can live like this for years, with just a helping of new compost on top now and again, and when the container is good and full it can make a lovely and unusual show when the flowers are open. This is also a very good way to show off the varieties with coloured or interestingly patterned leaves. If any plain throw-backs appear, weed them out. Celandines like sun when they are in full leaf and flower, but cool shade is good when they are dormant.

Silene dioica (Red Campion); *S. uniflora* (Sea Campion)

CARYOPHYLLACEAE *(Pink family)*,
subfamily 3 – CARYOPHYLLOIDEAE

This is a large genus with many species, some of which are familiar both as wild and garden plants. The 'Angel' Series of selections from the Mediter-

Cheerful if untidy
flowers of wild
Red Campion.

ranean *S. coeli-rosa* (Rose of Heaven) are popular annuals, while *S. schafta* has the RHS Award of Garden Merit as a rockery plant. Of our native species four have entries in the RHS *Encyclopedia of Garden Plants* (1996); they are *S. acaulis* (Moss Campion), *S. conica* (Sand Catchfly), *S. dioica* (Red Campion) and *S. uniflora* (Sea Campion). Moss Campion is a plant of mountain ledges and scree, and really requires specialist knowledge to grow well in lowland rock gardens, and Sand Catchfly is a rare annual flowering in summer, but Red Campion and Sea Campion are both good additions to the spring garden.

Red Campion must be one of the most abundant spring flowers, on hedge banks and roadsides, in woodland clearings and by tracks, among scrub and bracken. A mass of it in flower is a most cheering sight. A town visitor to the West Country, asking what it was and being told 'Pink Campion', beamed delightedly and said 'Ah, picnicking and camping', which seems a perfect distortion of this name! Growing naturally it is vigorous, and the flower stems flop untidily, so for the garden choose one of the selections, because they will behave in a more restrained way.

Some of the double forms such as 'Rosea Plena' and 'Richmond' have striking 'Ascot hat' flowers, while 'Thelma Kay' is even more outrageous, having variegated leaves as well. A form known wild in Shetland has particularly intense flower colour, and has already been brought into northern gardens, while a recent introduction, *S. dioica* 'Firefly', with the same brilliant colour, dark green leaves and a good upright habit is now widely available. It is still under Plant Breeders' Rights (PBR) so may not be propagated for sale except under licence. All the Red Campion forms need the same conditions, with decent soil that does not get too dry. They tolerate deciduous shade and are good in shrubberies, along hedges, and with ferns.

Sea Campion is a different style of plant and from quite a different habitat, but it too takes quite readily to life in the garden, and some attractive forms are available. It is a characteristic coastal plant, often growing with Thrift on rocks and shingle, sand and cliff ledges. Like Thrift it can tolerate extreme exposure, and can be found away from the sea on mountain gravels and toxic mine spoil, and is a pioneer plant in tundra habitats. Unlike the lush hairy leaves and stems of Red Campion, this plant is notably smooth and low-growing, and can be very pleasant on the rockery or between paving slabs, or in corners and on path edges in a gravel garden. Leaves are often glaucous (blue-grey or silvery), and it grows best in sunlight. Too much shade can green the leaves and cause the flowering stems to straggle. Wild plants often show variations in flower colour, from bright white to shades of pink. Some of these are the result of exposure or soil chemistry, but others stay true in cultivation.

As the flowers are enclosed in a most decorative inflated calyx (this is a close relative of the inland *Silene vulgaris*, Bladder Campion) the double Sea Campion with a posy of deeply-cut petals emerging from a delicious mottled and netted bladder is really charming. A well as 'Flore Pleno' and the pure white single 'Robin Whitebreast', the *Plant Finder* lists about half a dozen other varieties, so there is quite a choice. Being evergreen, at least in south Britain and Ireland, it is a useful plant for troughs, and of course goes naturally on a background of pretty pebbles.

Viola odorata
(Sweet Violet); *V. riviniana*
(Common Dog Violet)

VIOLACEAE *(Violet family)*

County flower of Lincolnshire:
Common Dog Violet

These tiny plants, in particular the Sweet Violet, carry quite a weight of symbolism and of literature (both artistic and botanical). Their distinctive flower shape makes them instantly recognizable in paintings (from Botticelli's *Primavera* to the medieval style 'flowery meads' surrounding figures in Burne-Jones' Pre-Raphaelite paintings), and they can be seen in the intricate 'mille-fleurs' tapestries woven in the late fifteenth century. In written imagery they are associated with meek, retiring ways, and many poetic references confirm this: Shakespeare in *A Winter's Tale* calls them

Sweet Violets cross-pollinate in the garden to produce new colours.

'... violets dim / But sweeter than the lids of Juno's eyes' and in *A Midsummer Night's Dream* they are the 'nodding violet'. John Donne in his poem 'The Ecstasy' mentions 'the violet's reclining head' and Wordsworth uses the plant to convey untouched innocence in 'She dwelt among the untrodden ways', when he describes the young girl Lucy as 'A violet by a mossy stone / Half hidden from the eye'. In the Victorian language of flowers, following the popular perception, the purple Sweet Violet stood for 'modesty', but the *white* Sweet Violet stood for 'faithfulness', which perhaps gives a clue to another quality of these plants (and one of more practical relevance to gardeners), which is persistence.

In country gardens, particularly in the past, violets are likely to have been present whether they had been planted or not. Both Sweet Violet and Common Dog Violet are widespread throughout Britain and Ireland, except in some mountain districts of the extreme west and north, and as their habitat includes field banks, hedgerows, roadsides and managed woods, all within easy reach of houses, they probably popped up here and there frequently. Sweet Violet also has its irresistible scent, so must have been moved into millions of gardens whether cottage or castle. It grows wild right across Europe, and throughout history has had many uses, for medicine, perfume and flavouring (the flowers are edible, and delicious candied). According to Theophrastus (371–287 BC), a pupil of Aristotle and sometimes called 'the Father of Botany', violets specially grown in the fields of Attica could be bought in the market in Athens. It must always have been one of the best known plants on this continent. Even recent garden writers seem to accept its presence in gardens as a basic necessity. Walter Ingwersen (1951) wrote, 'We would not be without [Sweet Violets] and welcome self-started colonies which appear here and there'. Graham Stuart Thomas, not noted for his tolerance, found them a bit small, but acknowledged their charm 'for naturalizing under shrubs' (1976). Christopher Lloyd (2000) praised both Sweet Violet and Common Dog Violet for being good 'fillers' in borders, for their shade tolerance under deciduous shrubs, and for 'looking nice poking out under hedge bottoms'. Their hardiness and wide range of tolerance (they will grow in almost any soil, in sun or shade) is enhanced by their curious flowering and fruiting techniques.

Sweet Violets are usually seen with abundant leaves. Keats noticed this, calling them 'Fast fading violets covered up in leaves' ('Ode to a Nightingale') and 'That queen of secrecy, the violet' ('Blue Ode'), and some gardeners who grow the wild forms try to establish them in lawns or on sunny banks where exposure will encourage them to flower above their leaves (surprisingly they thrive self-seeded into gravel paths). In more shady situations the leaves grow taller than the flowers and hide them. When violets were grown near Penzance in the early twentieth century, for cutting for the London market, pictures of the time show them in open sunny fields. In natural habitat this tall leaf growth may make it difficult for pollinators to spot the flowers, so Sweet Violets have a back-up strategy. After the main season is over, probably in late April, the plants produce a very different-looking flower, a twisted little greenish object with hardly any petals and short stems barely raising it off the ground.

This is the 'cleistogamous' flower, which does not have to open to attract insects because it is self-fertile, and will set seed inside its little secret wrapping. So if the plant has had no pollinators (or if somebody has picked all the flowers!) the plant can still reproduce, though these seeds will effectively be producing clones without the possible benefits brought by out-breeding.

Given that Sweet Violets can seed themselves so effectively, and both this species and the Common Dog Violet also spread enthusiastically by runners, introducing them into small modern gardens does need to be an informed decision. Unless you have a wild garden, large shrubbery or outside hedge, violets can become too abundant, and they are not easy to weed out. If you long for the scent, for that moment when a dozen flowers brought in on a cold winter day begins to warm up on your desk or kitchen table, one way to get round the problem is to collect some of the rarer varieties or cultivars, which will almost inevitably be less vigorous, or even grow some of the less hardy 'Parma' violets in a cold-frame. Since about 2000 there has been a revival of interest in historic and collectors' violets, and there are a number of specialist nurseries.

Recommended variants of the basic 'wild' forms are fairly easy to come by. Because of our historic fondness for Sweet Violets, they are as often naturalized as wild in the modern countryside, and they are also very often given and exchanged by gardeners. As well as blue/purple and white, the pink 'Rosea' Group is fairly often available. Nearly all violet species are notably promiscuous, so if you plant several colours, more shades will soon follow, and the prettiest can be selected for keeping.

If you are interested in decorative qualities more than in fragrance there is a readily available form of the scentless Common Dog Violet which is often sold as *V. labradorica*. This is actually pretty well a nonsense name, and what you will get is *V. riviniana* 'Purpurea' Group, an excellent garden plant if you are prepared for its invasiveness. The flowers are the usual rather china blue, while leaves and stems are lovely dark shades. It makes a striking foil for early daffodils, or under flowering shrubs. There is also a delightful pink-flowered form of *V. riviniana*, which is mysteriously nameless and unmentioned in most of the literature, though it wanders round local plant sales in some parts of the country. *V.canina* (Dog Violet) is quite an uncommon plant, and is not discussed here.

Additional spring wild flowers for possible garden use

Kidney Vetch with garden Wallflower 'Constant Cheer'.

Anthyllis vulneraria (Kidney Vetch)

Easily grown in sunny, well-drained soils, but rather straggly in the garden with dull colouring as the flowers die off. The bright red variant *A. vulneraria* ssp. *vulneraria* var. *coccinea* which is occasionally seen wild, and may be found on specialist seed lists, is good for rockeries or gravel gardens, or allowed to loll out of a trough. It usually seeds true.

Aquilegia vulgaris (Columbine)

The original native 'Granny's Bonnet' is single, short spurred and dark blue, but there are now so many varieties and escapes that columbines are best treated as garden plants.

Barbarea spp. (Winter Cresses)

Usually found as weeds of open ground and cultivations, these yellow-flowered cresses are sometimes brought into the garden for use in winter salads. Their rather tough dark green leaves have a good peppery taste to make greenhouse lettuce more interesting, and they are extremely hardy. Garden selections are available from seed lists.

Bellis perennis (Daisy)

If you like wild flowers, you have probably already encouraged this in your lawn, where it will flower (if it gets a chance) all year round. It is the first and most important 'flowery lawn' plant – masses of open flowers are an archetypal cheering sight, and in dull weather the pink tips of the closed petals are visible. Some enchanting variants are occasionally found and collected, with more colour than usual or double

'Daisy, Daisy…' A wonderful natural lawn in the Hebrides.

flowers, but unfortunately it is difficult to get hold of them, and even more difficult to keep them alive.

Chelidonium majus
(Greater Celandine)

This rather untidy plant is an ancient introduction; the burning orange latex that oozes out of its stalks if cut was once used for treating warts. It seeds freely, and the only form worth letting loose in the garden is one with double flowers.

Chrysosplenium alternifolium
(Alternate-leaved Golden Saxifrage)

This is not immediately recognizable as a Saxifrage, because it grows in wet semi-shade and has little flat umbels of flowers. It is widespread on shady stream sides and in boggy woodland, forming dense mats of leaves covered with gold flowers in March. If you have plenty of space on a shady pond edge or in a bog garden it makes good ground cover. A Chinese species, *C. davidianum*, which grows in much the same style, is available from some nurseries.

Conopodium majus
(Earthnut, Pignut)

This delicate little white umbel, with leaves cut as fine as fennel and stems like thin florists' wire, would be a charming addition to a wild garden, a grass plot with bulbs or a shrubbery edge, but although the tuberous 'nuts' which give its name are quite easily dug up, an old tradition says that the plant will never grow in ground which has been cultivated. Whatever the truth of this, it is very seldom seen in gardens.

Cymbalaria muralis
(Ivy-leaved Toadflax)

This trailing plant with tiny violet and white flowers is extremely common growing on walls. If you need to soften hard landscaping, walls or steps, it may be possible to establish it in crevices. Various colour forms including white are available, and an Italian relative *C. pallida* is easy to grow and sometimes naturalized in Britain. *C. muralis* will flower all year unless knocked back by hard frost.

Erysimum cheiri syn. *Cheiranthus cheiri* (Wallflower)

Frequently established on walls, waste ground and cliffs near settlement, this is an ancestor of our garden wallflowers. With plain yellow flowers and rather scruffy perennial plants it is a pleasant enough denizen if it is already growing near your garden, but is hardly worth introducing. The historic double forms, 'Bloody Warrior' and 'Harpur Crewe', are both notoriously difficult to keep.

Euphorbia spp. (Spurges)

There are three spring-flowering perennial native

Cypress Spurge flowers make a bright setting for a variegated Dogwood.

spurges worth considering for the garden. *E. amyg-daloides* (Wood Spurge) is familiar in gardens both in its wild (sometimes purple-leaved) varieties, and as its Turkish-collected subspecies *robbii*, sometimes known as 'Mrs Robb's Bonnet' because the original plants are said to have come to England in her hatbox. The native form is a tall sub-shrub, up to 1m, with erect spikes of yellowish-green bracts and flowers. The 'Purpurea' selections which have purple or reddish leaves make wonderful spring foliage plants, but are prone to powdery mildew in summer. Plants are

Irish Spurge in its natural habitat.

selections such as 'Fen's Ruby' with red-tipped leaves are undeniably decorative.

Lysimachia nemorum (Yellow Pimpernel)

This is a close relative of *L. nummularia* (Creeping Jenny), which is familiar to most gardeners because the ubiquitous gold-leaved form is so often used in basket and patio plantings. These two creeping perennial species are somewhat similar (but quite unlike the tall *L. vulgaris*, Yellow Loosestrife), but *L. nemorum* is a woodlander rather than a plant of wet ground. The little starry flowers start coming out in April, and will go on through most of the summer. It is too inconspicuous for flower beds, but makes a nice addition to shady grass paths, or trailing among mixed ground cover in shade. An enchanting primrose-yellow form called 'Pale Star' is occasionally available.

Polygala calcarea (Chalk Milkwort)

This is a charming little plant with really intense dark blue flowers, but like other chalk specialist plants it is not always easy to establish. It is listed in the *Plant Finder* and a French introduction called 'Lillet' has the AGM award. If you garden on chalk, or have available limestone, it would be worth trying on a bare bank, outcrop or rockery. Other native species such as *P. serpyllifolia* (Heath Milkwort) and *P. vulgaris* (Common Milkwort) are too small and straggly to be worth growing unless you are lucky enough to get them into your lawn. All creep at ground level in short grass communities.

Potentilla neumanniana, syn.* P. tabernaemontani (Spring Cinquefoil)

The golden flower cups and distinct palmate dark green leaves are lovely if you see this uncommon plant growing wild on exposed slopes, perhaps on the Mendip hills. It is occasionally listed by specialist nurseries, and would probably do well on a sunny limestone rockery. However, all the creeping potentillas are inclined to creep too much in garden condi-

short-lived, but may seed. *E. amygdaloides* var. *robbiae* creeps about, may refuse to stay in groups as planted, and can be hard to weed out, but the contrast between its dark evergreen leaves and pale green flower spikes is beautiful. It can be tried in dark, difficult places and looks lovely with ferns. *E. hyberna* (Irish Spurge) is very rare except in southwest Ireland, and needs quite specialized habitats with high annual humidity levels. It is extremely beautiful, but not easy.

E. *cyparissias* (Cypress Spurge) is much more common in gardens than in wild places. It is a notorious thug, spreading uncontrollably, but also has great charm if you can manage to balance it with other competitive ground cover plants. The golden flowers are honey scented on sunny days, and cultivated

Spring Squill with a pink form of Common Milkwort on the Cornish coast.

tions, and may lose their crisp good looks. Growing Spring Cinquefoil in a trough or separate container for the first year or so might be prudent.

Sanicula europaea (Sanicle)

This curious little woodlander is actually an umbellifer, a member of the *Apiaceae* (carrot family), but looking at its rather lumpy little crowded brownish flower heads, this is quite difficult to guess. It has nice leaves, and is quite easily introduced to shady places with plenty of leaf mould, but its appeal is low key.

Scilla verna (Spring Squill)

County flower of Co. Down

This little bulb, one of our only two native squills, is one of the character plants of coastal Britain and Ireland, often seen in flowery carpets in cliff grassland with Milkworts and Thrift. If you look at it very closely, its pale blue petals with darker midribs and anthers, on dark stems, are beautiful, but as a garden plant it is outclassed in colour and showiness by many 'little blue bulbs', including some from its own genus and other groups such as *Chionodoxa* and *Ipheion*. It can of course be added to a well-drained sunny rockery (as can its autumn-flowering relative, *S. autumnalis*), but its modest charms are best seen in large populations.

LEFT: **Wild Tulip is rare now, but available from bulb catalogues.**
BELOW: **Spring Squill has elegant colouring.**

Stellaria holostea (Greater Stitchwort)

The white stars of this very common plant are one of the prettiest sights of early spring, growing with Celandines, Primroses and Red Campion on thousands of hedge banks and road verges. If you have any semi-wild areas such as rough banks or hedge bottoms in your garden it can be a pleasant addition, as it is reasonably unaggressive when mixed with other plants and grasses, and fades into the background when not in flower. It is too much of a straggler to be grown alone.

Tulipa sylvestris (Wild Tulip)

This very pretty little yellow tulip really hardly counts as a British wild flower. It is an ancient introduction, which has lost nearly all of its old naturalized sites to ploughing and improvement. However, it is readily available on bulb lists (though the name covers an unpredictable range of continental and cultivated forms), and is well worth trying naturalized with other bulbs in grass. The form known in England has rather gracefully narrow flowers.

Hawthorn is often called 'Mayflower' as in the familiar saying 'Cast not a clout 'ere May be out'. Its coming marks the end of the spring season.

SUMMER

The Lady's-mantles are a suitable genus to lead into the flowers of summer, because they typify the sort of contribution that wild flowers can make to gardens during this season. In early spring when ground is bare, bushes leafless and grass rather short, our native flowers look wonderful, in romantic drifts or making magic of hidden corners. In summer though, unless you can create bright masses of mixed cornfield annuals, many of our wild flowers look small, untidy or

OPPOSITE PAGE: *Umbilicus rupestris* **(Navelwort) self-seeded on a Canary Island Date Palm in Tresco Gardens.**
BELOW: **Art and nature – Lady's-mantle arranging itself in a Yorkshire garden.**

pale beside cultivated or imported plants. What they can do wonderfully though is provide green background and texture in more spectacular plantings. Both the photographs on these pages show this, and feature plants that are behaving as if they were wild, which is a key point in the kind of gardens which benefit from growing some native species. If your summer garden is planned and structured around bright and substantial cultivated plants, the addition of self-sown, less conspicuous flowers and annual grasses can add 'fill' and interest. Navelwort (opposite) is a true native, usually found in wall crevices or on scree and cliffs, but in Tresco finds an exotic but perfectly functional habitat, adding natural charm to an extremely high-profile garden. The Lady's-mantle

round the wall statue was originally an introduction, now very frequent indeed in gardens, and often found established outside them. It is included here as an example of 'wild' behaviour, and to show the possible charm and grace of chance sowings. This garden had been partly abandoned for some years with only the most basic management, and the beauty of this spontaneous development makes a very strong argument for tolerating some self-seeding. The hand of Fate can sometimes be as skilful as any top garden designer!

Alchemilla alpina (Alpine Lady's-mantle); *A. mollis* (Lady's-mantle)

ROSACEAE *(Rose family)*, subfamily 2 – ROSOIDEAE

Alchemilla mollis, introduced from the Carpathian mountains in Turkey as late as 1874 but now ubiquitous in gardens, is actually larger than almost any of our native species, which are a group of complicated little plants of upland meadows, very difficult to tell apart. Some gardeners detest its lavish seeding, but it has many excellent qualities too. Christopher Lloyd (2000) called it 'incredibly obliging, sowing itself into paving cracks, placing itself beneath garden seats...'. Admittedly Great Dixter has much more space than most gardens do, but he also praised the 'comfortable and settled look' which the clumps of softly hairy, shapely leaves provide as early as May, and he sensibly advised cutting them back to the ground in July (for fresh growth in autumn) and dead-heading to keep seeding in control. A beautiful quality of this species is the way the cupped leaves hold moisture, retaining 'light-reflecting water drops, after rain or dew, to look like quicksilver'. The sprays of tiny green flowers are immensely valuable in flower arranging, including making a soft setting for rose buds, which incredibly are their close cousins!

The native *A. alpina* (Alpine Lady's-mantle) is a smaller and daintier plant, with beautiful silver edges

Raindrops caught on Lady's-mantle leaves.

and backs to the leaflets. It is extremely attractive established on rockeries or in paving crevices, or in beds where it can be left undisturbed to develop its matted, almost woody clumps, and where the leaves can show up well. However, like most mountain plants it needs the right conditions, and will not flourish just anywhere. Walkers in Scotland sometimes use its first appearance as a clue to when they are approaching the altitude of 500m, so it is a real upland plant, and although it therefore needs light and sun, it also likes cool conditions, and moisture in the soil. It is listed by good alpine nurseries which will probably have another rather similar species too. *A. conjuncta* (Silver Lady's-mantle) has sometimes been found in natural habitat in the Scottish Borders and elsewhere, but there are usually suspicions that it has been planted, as it is really a native of the Pyrenees. Both these species have small greenish-yellow flowers, and will give interest through a long season if you can establish them where their matted growth will not interfere with other plants.

Leaves of Alpine Lady's-mantle have an elegant silver edge.

The delicious softness of Marsh-mallow leaves is matched by the plant's soothing properties.

Althaea officinalis (Marsh-mallow)

MALVACEAE *(Mallow family)*

This is never a common plant, and it comes from quite a specialized habitat, but it is so beautiful and has such a long history as a medicinal plant that it is worth trying to grow it in the garden. It is scattered round the coasts of Britain, found on the banks of brackish ditches in areas of saltings – it is a character plant for instance of the edges of the 'rhynes' in the Somerset Levels, and in the Thames grazing marshes. Grigson (1958) with his usual talent for drama, calls the tall, pink-flowered, velvet-leaved plants 'an exquisite surprise in muddy, salty, desolate, smelly surroundings'. Plants from this kind of habitat do not *need* any salt, though they can tolerate some, but they do cope well with occasional flooding (with either fresh or salt water), and need to grow where their roots are close to a consistent water table. In other words, don't let the plants suffer dry spells, but make sure they are planted in soil which retains moisture at least below ground. Soils also need to be quite nutritious, because the wild habitat is often enriched by silt left after winter floods.

Marshmallow sweets are now completely artificial, but they were formerly based on an extract of Marsh-mallow roots. The thick roots produce 'a clammie and slimy juice' (Gerard, 1597) which has starchy thickening properties, and is very soothing in many healing applications both internal and external. It was frequently used by conventional doctors and practitioners of folk medicine for conditions from the King's Evil (a tubercular swelling of the lymph glands) to sunburn. It is still sometimes recommended by herbalists to ease pain in conditions such as Irritable Bowel Syndrome – bits of the dried plant being made into a rather slimy but very soothing tea.

Decorating a desolate landscape, Marsh-mallow in the Thames marshes.

Worth close attention – the tiny Bog Pimpernel on bare, recently burned heath in Cornwall.

Anagallis tenella
(Bog Pimpernel)

PRIMULACEAE (Primrose family)

This enchanting little perennial is quite common throughout Britain and Ireland growing in bogs, flushes and damp unimproved grassland, but its tiny size and creeping habit make it quite difficult to find unless in flower, and few people bother to bring it into the garden. If the scale of your patch is small though, and in particular if you like growing special plants in containers, the Bog Pimpernel is worth considering. In its natural habitat it is usually seen creeping through much heftier plants, and is therefore inconspicuous, but occasionally a piece of damp bare ground where a path has been altered, or where tall heath or bushes have been burnt, allows it to grow without competition for a while. A tight clump develops which can become completely covered with flowers, and looks like a star plant for a damp rockery or gravelly pool edge. Bog Pimpernel can also be grown in a shallow clay pan standing in a dish or tray of water, and looks extremely pretty when its runners begin to trail over the sides. Use a soil-based compost,

and rain water for the tray, and your 'bog in a pot' should otherwise be no trouble. A light sunny position is needed for good flowering. A deep pink selection, named 'Studland' after the part of Dorset where it was originally found, has the AGM award and is sometimes listed by specialist nurseries.

Artemesia absinthum
(Wormwood)

ASTERACEAE, syn. COMPOSITAE
(Daisy family), subfamily 2 – ASTEROIDEAE

Many, many varieties, species, hybrids and selections of the *Artemesia* genus are used in modern gardens. Some are tall sub-shrubs reaching a metre or more, others are almost prostrate, and a large percentage of them have the fine, silvery foliage which is characteristic, and makes them very popular. This type of foliage, with the silver colour provided by close-set thin hairs, is developed by plants to protect them from extremes of temperature and exposure, hot and cold. Temperate Britain does not have much need for

Pale and interesting – leaves and flowers of Wormwood.

Like most of the genus it is aromatic when crushed, and has historical importance because of its use in making absinthe. Although this name has a romantic aura connected with the poets and painters who were addicted to it, the drink was extremely dangerous. Wormwood oil is corrosive, as well as hallucinogenic, so both body and brain can be severely damaged. In Britain it had more mundane uses, to make a horridly bitter medicine to dispel worms, and as a strewing herb to deter fleas.

Campanula glomerata (Clustered Bellflower); C. latifolia (Giant Bellflower); C. patula (Spreading Bellflower); C. rotundifolia (Harebell); C. trachelium (Nettle-leaved Bellflower)

CAMPANULACEAE (Bellflower family)

County flower of Rutland: Clustered Bellflower; Co. Antrim and Dumfriesshire: Harebell

As we know, the effects of the ice ages left Britain and Ireland with very small floras compared to continental countries. In a large genus, such as *Campanula* or *Geranium*, there are many more species in Europe than here, but a considerable number of them grow in temperate areas with climates not essentially very different from ours. Alpine meadows, for instance, seem very foreign set below snowy peaks, but many of the species in those flowery swards are similar or identical to some of our wild flowers, and share much the same kind of soils and climate. This means that gardeners have had a large reservoir of species to collect, select and breed from, all of which will grow easily here, and this is why the bellflowers are so important in our gardens. It also means that introduced species naturalize readily, and some have been established for many years. These include: *C. alliarifolia* (Cornish Bellflower), a rather floppy but pleasing

this strategy, but we do have one native species which is handsome enough for the garden. Wormwood has silvery-green leaves and stems, and tall spikes of little bead-like yellow flowers which make a lovely and unusual addition to flower arrangements.

In the garden Wormwood is a long-lived perennial, and although it eventually forms substantial clumps it is not nearly as rampant as its much plainer green-leaved relative *A. vulgaris* (Mugwort), which has a dazzling variegated selection called 'Oriental Lime-light' and must be kept trapped in a strong container. Flowers are usually out in July and August, and dead-heading will bring fresh growth in autumn. The silvery leaves will look good for about eight months in average years. A sunny spot is essential, but poor or stony soil is fine, so Wormwood can be useful in borders, shrubbery edges and gravel gardens.

LEFT: Harebells grow in many habitats, here on karst limestone in the Burren.
BELOW: A white form of Giant Bellflower by a castle ruin in Northumberland.

cream-flowered species, good on rough banks and shrubbery edges; *C. lactiflora* (Milky Bellflower), very tall, to 2m, and lovely, with some excellent garden selections; *C. persicifolia* (Peach-leaved Bellflower), familiar garden plant and escape on walls and dry banks – look for white and semi-double 'cup-and-saucer' cultivars; *C. rapunculoides* (Creeping Bellflower), lovely spikes of dark blue bells, but hopelessly invasive; *C. rapunculus* (Rampion Bellflower), once grown as a root vegetable, now rare but occasionally available from specialist seed lists; and of course the ubiquitous wall and rockery creepers *C. poscharskyana* (Trailing Bellflower) and *C. portenschlagiana* (Adria Bellflower), which decorate so many present-day streets.

The five species listed at the top of this section are true natives, and all make worthy garden plants. Christopher Lloyd (2000) wrote 'It would be difficult to be unkind about the bellflowers, which are a particularly graceful lot... with colouring that does not disturb the sensitive', and he grew almost all the natives at Great Dixter.

C. latifolia (Giant Bellflower) is a northern species in Britain, and not native in Ireland. It grows on wood edges, rough banks and along rivers, and will tolerate some shade. The upward-tilted bells can be varying colours from almost white to purplish-blue (some lovely forms have whitish flowers freckled with deepest purple, with dark stems and bracts). There are a number of good named selections, like the classic 'Brantwood' which has very rich colouring. The straight stems, up to 1.2m, make it a very good back-of-border flower, or placed among shrubs, though the flowering season only lasts through the midsummer weeks. Just remember its north-country origins, and plant it where it can find a cool root-run, and not get too scorched or dry.

C. trachelium (Nettle-leaved Bellflower) is another tallish species that will grow in light shade. It is more inclined to flop than the Giant Bellflower, and the flowers are nearly always a rather pale blue, so it is more suitable for wild garden or shrubbery than for a border. It also really hates being dry – although in Britain it can usually be found along wood edges or on old hedge banks, in Ireland (where it is much rarer) its usual habitat is swamp woodland or the banks of large rivers. There are two really delightful garden forms: 'Bernice' is a soft violet double, and quite widely available; 'Alba Flore Pleno' is much harder to source, but well worth the hunt. Both these usually grow rather shorter than the wild plant, and do need care and attention. Plant them in soil with some leaf mould, and make sure that they have enough moisture in dry weather. They are exquisite in a shade garden with ferns and heucheras.

C. glomerata (Clustered Bellflower) comes from a different habitat, mostly in the south of England, on chalk downs and open calcareous pastures. The plant communities which make up these sometimes very ancient downland turfs are very intricate, with herbs and grasses tightly knitted together. The competitive strategies and balances between plants already under pressure from grazing are complicated and impossible to replicate in the garden, and this does mean that a single species removed from that matrix may behave unpredictably. In the field this plant looks most desirable, with quite neat dark basal leaves and stiff upright stalks to 50cm, topped by clusters of intensely rich purple flowers. However, in the garden, unchecked by competition, it becomes

Clustered Bellflower is compact and colourful.

'uncomfortably invasive', spreading so that it 'chokes itself into starvation almost immediately' and 'flowering becomes sparse' (Lloyd, 2000). The answer is to divide plants as often as you can (just after flowering is good), replanting the splits into rich soil. This principle can also work if you grow it as a container plant – a good pot-full looks terrific, and will flower for a long season if you dead head – tipping the plants out each year, dividing and repotting into fresh compost. Sun and light are essential, and this species is rather more drought tolerant than the Giant or Nettle-leaved Bellflowers. 'Superba' is a good large-flowered selection, while 'Caroline' has flowers of a magical greyish-pink.

C. patula (Spreading Bellflower) has yet another place of interest in the garden, but it also has more problems than the former species, and can be difficult to establish. It is an annual or biennial (germinating

Spreading Bellflower is worth encouraging.

though, and available from specialist seed lists, so worth experimenting with.

Oddly enough the native campanula with the widest range of tolerance, and the very easiest to grow, is the frail-looking Harebell (called 'Bluebell' in Scotland). The Latin specific name *rotundifolia* seems somewhat bizarre until you have grown the plant yourself. What you see on the fine flowering stems are tiny linear leaves like scraps of grass or pine needles, and 'round-leaved' seems a nonsensical label. However, the basal leaves, hidden in surrounding grass, and often shrivelled away by flowering time, are truly round. Plants in the garden seed well, and this shape is the secret for saving the seedlings from being pulled out, as the tiny plantlets have recognizable circular leaves. Harebells need a reasonably airy spot where they will get sun, but they are not fussy about soils, and are of course very hardy. One thing to keep in mind is that plants that thrive in places with a high rainfall, such as northwest Scotland, may actually still prefer decent drainage. Harebells often grow on rock ledges or stony slopes, where even if masses of rain falls it keeps on the move, dripping downhill, so there is no question of this being a bog plant. A white form is sometimes available (though it is unlikely to seed true), and the plant is a delight in many types of planting, on the rockery, in a trough, by paths and at the edge of borders.

opportunistically in both autumn and spring), and if it is happy will seed itself around most prettily, its thin upright stalks causing no interference to other plants. It is quite rare as a wild flower in England now, because it used to grow in open clearings and rides in worked woodland, most of which are now too overgrown. A nationally important population in Surrey used to persist beside a major railway line where track maintenance and management of the banks kept the habitat open. Walter Ingwersen (1951) records his affection for the species, having seen it in 'untold thousands' in alpine meadows, but wrote that he always 'failed to make it at home' in his garden. 'I have never managed to get a massed effect with it, only isolated plants, and these now seed themselves among my pot plants rather than where I desire them to grow', and this may well describe the most likely result of sowing it. It is astonishingly beautiful

Chamerion angustifolium, syn. *Epilobium angustifolium* (Rosebay Willowherb)

ONAGRACEAE *(Willowherb family)*

County flower of London

Because it rapidly colonizes disturbed ground, where its spreading roots can make huge patches, this is one of the most widely known wild flowers. Its brilliant colour is eyecatching, sometimes lighting up ugly and derelict land. It famously appeared in the ruins of bombed London after the Second World War, and is

something of an icon for hope and revival. It is some-times called 'Fireweed' because it thrives on recently burnt ground. Garden writers agree on its looks but regret its invasiveness. 'A plant of marvellous beauty, but of impossibly invasive habit for the garden, how-ever glorious it may be on waste ground' (Thomas, 1976). This is echoed by Christopher Lloyd (2000): 'Its tall racemes of bright carmine flowers are a great sight in July...', and he comments on how the flower colour is beautifully repeated in the developing seed heads, but he admits that its uncontrollable spread 'is not a recipe which will appeal to any but the most slovenly gardener'.

Part of the trouble is that the plant seeds lavishly, as well as spreading vigorously by roots. The plumed air-borne seeds can almost look like mist when carried by autumn breezes. Walter Ingwersen (1951) gives the

TOP: Hopeful or horrible? Attitudes differ on Rosebay Willowherb.
ABOVE: Rosebay Willowherb attracts many pollinators.

Sea Kale on a shingle beach in Co. Kerry.

same praise and the same cautions, but also says, 'It is perfectly lovely among Birches', suggesting that this natural effect could be repeated in the garden. If you have room for Silver Birches, and the time to dead head before seeds ripen on the Rosebay Willowherb, this is indeed a tempting model. There are several garden selections available which behave less aggressively, but unfortunately the white form with its green stems and seed pods can look rather dreary. A recent selection called 'Stahl Rose' is much prettier, having very pale pink flowers and red stems. It was promoted as ideal for the Piet Oudolf style of massed 'prairie' plantings, but it is actually not at all easy to keep. This is a beautiful species though, and worth approaching with courage and imagination *if* you have plenty of space.

Crambe maritima (Sea Kale)

BRASSICACEAE, formerly CRUCIFERAE – *(Cabbage family)*

'Wild flower' is too pale a term for this magnificent plant, which has grandeur and presence but also beauty in its smallest details. It is, however, seldom seen in modern gardens, and there are several reasons for this. Primarily, it has become regrettably rare on the shingle beaches of Britain and Ireland (where it survives this difficult habitat), so most people don't know what it looks like. If it persists in the consciousness of a few gardeners, it is probably as a vegetable which has long been out of fashion. *Crambe cordifolia*, a spectacular relative introduced to gardens from the Caucasus, is now a much more familiar plant than our wonderful native.

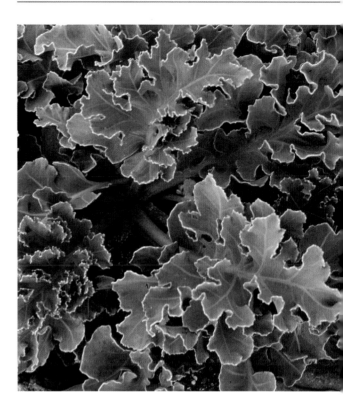

ABOVE: **Sea Kale buds and stems have beautiful colour.**
LEFT: **Both Sea Kale and Rhubarb can be blanched under pots.**

The main reason for its decline in the wild is probably simply the modern pressure on beaches – shingle extraction, sea defences, marina developments and leisure activities have probably all had their part. The stems (rather than the leaves) are a delicious vegetable, and throughout history people have collected them to eat. There are many accounts of the way that sand or shingle can be heaped up to blanch the spring growth, and of it being sold in coastal markets, but this must have proved sustainable for many centuries and the 1970s' craze for wild foods cannot really be blamed for Sea Kale's current rarity. It was also grown in gardens: as early as 1799 the great botanist William Curtis published a pamphlet on how to cultivate it as a vegetable, and most garden manuals, at least up to about 1920, included such advice. Ironically, it is probably this popularity which led to its current obscurity.

Establishing this plant as a crop does take some effort, and because of its unusual deliciousness, and the fact that only the young stems are eaten, it became a luxury vegetable. Commercial growers concentrated on producing the blanched stems earlier and earlier in the year, forcing them in dark, frost free sheds. Out in the garden, plants used to be heaped with cinders or shavings to 'bring them up', or covered by pots similar to those used for Rhubarb.

The plants are very long-lived, but have to be grown in deep drills, filled with sand or gravel well mixed with manure or other organic material. Shingle beach plants have to have substantial roots to stop them being torn out by storms, but although the habitat looks poor, beaches get all kinds of good nutrients from rotted seaweed and dead creatures, so this species has to be well fed. To get the best of the subtle taste of the stems (steamed like asparagus and

Sea Kale in flower – stems curve sideways not up, avoiding the fiercest wind forces.

eaten with Hollandaise sauce or melted butter) they must be picked and cooked on the same day. They have no 'shelf life' and become floppy and tasteless after a few hours, so Sea Kale is worthless in terms of supermarket trade. Before Constance Spry broke a major style barrier in the 1930s and '40s, by using vegetables in flower arrangements, the divide between the kitchen garden and the flower borders was pretty fixed, so there was no natural progression for this plant from vegetable to ornamental, and it became forgotten in the shift to smaller, less labour-intensive gardens.

There is no reason though why even small gardens should not have one or two plants. Once the ground is prepared, a yearly feed or two is all that is necessary, and eating it or not can be a personal choice. Graham Stuart Thomas, often quite a dry character, wrote admiringly (1976) that Sea Kale has 'perhaps the most beautiful of all large glaucous leaves, the wide blades are exquisitely carved and lobed .... The knobs of purple growth emerging from the soil are a joy to see and to eat in the spring.' He also commented on the value of both leaves and the large heads of honey-scented white flowers for cutting.

The round, jade-green seed capsules are also unusual and decorative. Leaves die back in autumn, and any litter can be cleared in early spring so that bulbs can be grown quite close by to flower and give interest to the 'footprint' of the Sea Kale before its own growth begins to show in April.

Deptford Pink is protected in this old railway cutting.

Dianthus armeria (Deptford Pink); D. deltoides (Maiden Pink); D. gratianopolitanus (Cheddar Pink)

CARYOPHYLLACEAE (Pink family)

County flower of Roxburghshire: Maiden Pink; Somerset: Cheddar Pink

Compared with the well-known and historic pinks and carnations of gardens, our wild members of this genus are small fry. There is something irresistibly appealing about this group of plants though. They have been appreciated for centuries, and still are, as two out of three species above have been voted county flowers. These three are also our only natives – many wild pinks are either alpine plants, or prefer Mediterranean conditions, so Britain is too damp and sunless for them. Two continental pinks, both highly scented, which have contributed to the breeding of garden pinks, are naturalized on old walls in a few places where they have been for centuries. D. caryophyllus (Clove Pink) is still known for instance on the walls of Rochester Castle, where it may have arrived with the stone imported by the Normans to build their fortress. It is treasured by local residents. D. plumarius (Pink) is similarly established at Beaulieu Abbey, though here it is more likely to have been brought by Cistercian monks to scent their garden.

The so-called Deptford Pink is more of an oddity. It is little known except by the conservation botanists who try to prevent it becoming extinct in Britain (it has only once been found in Ireland and its status there has never become clear). It is an annual or biennial, standing up to 25cm tall in good conditions, with tiny bright carmine flowers on branching wiry stems, so looks very different from its relatives which are perennials, their larger flowers held above neat

Cheddar Pinks at home in Cheddar Gorge.

natural habitat is on open sandy ground, and for centuries it probably grew mostly at the edge of tracks and arable fields. Modern tidiness and intensive farming have obliterated many marginal habitats, others have been developed, and the plant is now extremely rare and threatened, surviving in sites such as an old railway bank where well-disposed people maintain the open conditions necessary. It does, however, take perfectly to garden conditions if you are prepared to let it seed around, coming up in gravel and between paving stones, or scattered in flower beds and containers. It is a very discreet denizen in these conditions, never causing problems for other plants. The new leaf rosettes in spring or autumn are neat and shapely (and easy to recognize after your first year of growing) and are not difficult to move when they are young, or to weed away. The basal leaves die off during the flowering season, and one of the Deptford Pink's great charms is its ability to surprise. It may grow quite unnoticed among other plants, the rosette almost gone, and the flower stems thinner than a blade of grass and very hard to spot. Then the brilliant little flowers begin to open, making sparks of carmine opening a few at a time for months on end. Plants on gravel may get walked on, in which case it will flower at ground level on a tiny tuft of leaves.

Obviously such an inconspicuous plant does not get mentioned in garden literature, but if it is allowed to get going in a garden so that little sparks show up in unexpected places for months on end, it can bring great enjoyment, and always produces enough seed to pass on to friends. Please don't scatter it in the countryside though – records which may come from deliberately sown plants cause huge problems to conservationists. Always ask about the origin too if you buy seed – even that available from specialist lists may well be from abroad, so should not be let loose in the British countryside.

The Maiden Pink and the Cheddar Pink both make sweet garden plants, and can be used much more formally than the Deptford Pink. They both make good rockery plants, gradually increasing to form nice patches and cushions, can be added to alpine troughs, and the Cheddar Pink can be used as an edging. Being good in gardens has been bad for this plant

cushions of leaves. Even its name is a mistake. Gerard published the name in his *Herball* in 1597, but it was attached to the wrong plant. The description of the pink in 'the great field next to Deptford' was clearly of the Maiden Pink. This seems to have been forgotten though, and when in 1633 Thomas Johnson published a good picture of the 'Deptford Pink' showing *D. armeria* this pairing has stuck ever since, even though the plant may never have grown in SE8! Its

in its only native locality in the Cheddar Gorge, because it used to be dug up for sale to tourists. Like the Killarney Fern in Killarney, there are heart-breaking accounts of local people selling baskets of roots at the railway station, which is why visitors now can really only use binoculars to see flowers on the most inaccessible crags, and the species is legally protected. Obviously if your rockery has limestone rocks the plant will feel at home, but in general if it has sun and good drainage it will tolerate most garden conditions. All pinks are fussy (though some bred recently are less so), but if they 'do' in your garden, so will the Cheddar Pink. It can be sourced from specialist nurseries.

The Maiden Pink is uncommon, without being a national rarity, and can occasionally be found in thin, open grassland communities, often on sandy soils. It has much more colour variation than the previous

Bright eyes – a wild form of the variable Maiden Pink.

two species. Robert Gathorne-Hardy (1961) grew forms 'from white through strawberries-and-cream to a dark purplish-red'. The flowers are smaller than those of the Cheddar Pink, but appear in good numbers. The plants may not be very long-lived, but seedlings appear to keep up the appearance of a spreading patch. It may also seed pleasantly into gravel or turf. Sun and good drainage are essential. There are some excellent nursery selections available, the best known probably being 'Brilliant' and 'Leuchtfunk' ('Flashing Light'). The species itself has the AGM.

Foxgloves on an Exmoor hedge.

Digitalis purpurea (Foxglove)

SCROPHULARIACEAE *(Figwort family)*

County flower of Argyllshire, Birmingham, Leicestershire and Monmouthshire

Ever since our ancestors started to cut trees and clear land, the Foxglove must have been one of the best known of all wild flowers. Its size and colour make it impossible to miss, and it thrives on disturbance, so the clearance of the wildwood in prehistoric times would have suited it well. Now it is frequent on road verges and hedge banks, in new plantations and clearings in mature woodland, as well as in rough bracken areas and scrub. Its seeds remain viable for years, so even if surrounding vegetation becomes too thick and shady for the plants, after clearance by cutting or burning the Foxgloves quickly germinate again. This species is biennial, forming a leaf rosette in its first year, and the tall flowering spike in the second summer. After seeding the plant dies, but if conditions are suitable there will be many new plantlets appearing the next year.

Grigson (1958) collected more than a hundred local names. A large number of them are variations on a few themes (foxes, dogs, fingers, gloves, thimbles), while others are often connected with witches, elves and goblins. 'Foxglove' itself is one of the oldest, *foxes glōfa* in Old English. The plant also has a rich history of medical use. In folk medicine its uses must have

Foxgloves in the 'giant spotted' group have striking patterns, which also guide bees into the bells.

been of a 'kill or cure' nature, because the leaves contain powerful drugs that can be deadly in the wrong dose. Over time though preparations became particularly associated with the treatment of dropsy (the old name for many soft-tissue swellings now distinguished as different kinds of oedema), which was actually very close to the mark because oedemas are caused by congestive heart failure. *Digitalis* species contain the active principles digoxin and digitoxin, which are still used in important heart medicines. The scientific link between witches' brew and modern medicine was the research of William Withering, a doctor and botanist, who published his key findings in *An Account of the Foxglove* in 1785.

It may not sound romantic, but the primary use of Foxgloves in the garden is as a wonderfully useful experimental tool. Because they are biennials, they can be looking spectacular only a year after you have made a plan, painted an imaginary garden picture; and because they are biennials, if your idea is not a success they can be gone with no effort before their seeds set. They can be used to give height in slow-growing new plantings; they can be grouped to assess a colour statement; they can tone beautifully with peonies in a June border; they can be planted singly or scattered to provide verticals in soft grass or fern plantings; they can make a raw new bank or bed or terrace look lovely while you work out how to develop the long-term planting scheme. Although in the wild they are abundant on acid soils, they will tolerate most types in the garden, and are really very low maintenance. Some lovely colour forms are available, as seed and sometimes as young plants, and once you have them growing you can encourage your favourites. They can be left to seed in situ, or you can collect pods for spring sowing outdoors. They breed reasonably true (rogues can always be weeded out), and seedlings move perfectly well during their first year. They will grow in sun or dappled shade (white forms are wonderful for lighting up shrubberies), but deep shade defeats them.

Dipsacus fullonum (Wild Teasel); *D. pilosus* (Small Teasel)

DIPSACACEAE *(Teasel family)*

The Wild Teasel is a marginal plant, growing beside roads, rivers and railways, at the edge of fields and woods, even in trading estates and by rubbish dumps. As it is often seen in rough habitats and waste ground where its sturdy plants can become very numerous, and because it is an efficient self-seeder, it

The fascinating 'blue belt' pattern of opening Wild Teasel florets.

is mostly left out of gardening books – too common in all senses, and a vigorous 'weed'. It does, however, have an entry in the *RHS A to Z*, and some writers have rejected this reputation for vulgarity. Walter Ingwersen (1951) who was quite an arbiter of garden taste wrote, 'I always think the common Teasel... an extraordinarily stately and effective plant... The foliage is bold and striking and the upper leaves are stem-clasping and form jagged-edged cups around the flowering stems, which often hold water...'. The latter feature is fascinating, because insects drown in

Wild teasel plants are excellent in the Autumn garden.

leaves are distinct from an early age, so weeding out or moving young plants is easy. They love difficult clay soils, and do not need feeding. Almost their most valuable time is in autumn and winter, when the plant is dead and brown but the fine branched plants still stand upright, making excellent silhouettes among tall autumn grasses, or behind Michaelmas Daisies and hardy Chrysanthemums. Goldfinches really do like the seeds, so a plant or two close to a window can provide delightful chance views. The heads are invaluable for flower arrangements (dried stems last well) or even for making toy hedgehogs for Christmas!

Our other native teasel, *D. pilosus* (Small Teasel), is much less common, found only occasionally on the edges of damp woodland, in hedgerows and on wooded stream banks in England. It is not a grand or statuesque plant, being much smaller in all its parts and having a rather lax, untidy habit. The heads are small and round (though still having the wonderful spiny construction) and the flowers are creamy and inconspicuous. It does, however, have great charm as a shrubbery plant or in hedges. The little heads appear in profusion, while the leaves and stems will 'disappear' into any surrounding greenery, and be propped up by nearby shrubs or fences. It dies off in autumn in the same way as its larger relative, the

these cups, and there has been speculation that the plant is in the process of evolving an ability to digest these spare nutrients. Most of the architectural appeal of the Wild Teasel is in its stature and the wonderful spiny curves of bract surrounding the fir-cone-shaped heads, but these heads are also appealing in flower, because the myriad florets do not all open at once, but form a surprising blue belt round the head.

Like Foxgloves, these are biennials, but once established in the garden they will appear here and there, or can be sown for effect in their second summer. The

The dainty round heads of Small Teasel grow in profusion.

heads drying to a rather lighter brown and having a very pretty airy appearance. Without winning any prizes for neatness or shapely plant form, this is a delightful and unusual species for a cool shrubbery, informal bank or damp shady pool side.

Eryngium maritimum
(Sea Holly)

APIACEAE, syn. UMBELLIFERAE
(Carrot family), subfamily 2 – SANICULOIDEAE

County flower of Liverpool

This genus is extremely well known and popular in gardens. From the intense colours of modern selections such as *E. bourgatii* 'Picos Amethyst' or *E. × zabellii* 'Jos Eijking' to the pale elegance of *E. giganteum* ('Miss Wilmott's Ghost' – the queen of self-seeders), almost every garden has a representative. Many cultivars are derived from continental (in particular Mediterranean) species, but our own *E. maritimum* is a plant of the western seaboards of Europe, including southern Scandinavia, so needs less heat and sun than some of the more fashionable plants. It grows at the back of sand and shingle beaches, and on sand dunes, round almost the whole of Britain and Ireland, except for Scotland and parts of northeast England, though it has declined due to modern pressure on beaches. Plants are low-growing, and very deep rooted – sensible strategies for a plant of stormy and

Sea Holly can do well in sunny gardens.

An effective 'beach' planting designed by Piet Oudolf includes *Eryngium* species.

unstable habitat. The stiff foliage is the most beautiful pale blue-green with silver veins, with the warmer blue-purple flowers held close above the leaves.

It will grow in most gardens with good light and sun, so long as the soil is prepared with added sand and gravel to a depth of at least 60cm, to give the long roots proper drainage. The fleshy roots were formerly dug and boiled with sugar and orange-flower water to make a sweet, which was supposed to be good for restoring energy, as well as being a treat. Colchester was known for its 'candied eringoes' from Tudor times until the nineteenth century.

Euphorbia lathyris (Caper Spurge); *E. serratula*, syn.* *E. stricta* (Upright Spurge, Tintern Spurge)

EUPHORBIACEAE *(Spurge family)*

These two annual/biennial spurges are perhaps an acquired taste. Like a number of other plants in this book, they are recommended for their natural opportunism and ability to seed around, so they are very difficult to manage in a precise planting plan. If young plants are introduced in a design they will flower there that summer but will come up in different places in the garden next year. If you enjoy chance effects these are both attractive and unusual plants, making stylish individual contributions.

The Caper Spurge is possibly native, and certainly very widely found as an escape. It seems to attract misleading information: most importantly it is not a source for capers. The seed heads look rather like the buds preserved for seasoning, but these come from quite a different plant, *Capparis spinosa*, which does not grow in western Europe. The word 'spurge' comes from the Latin *expurgare*, so means a plant that purges, and this one was used as a laxative in early medicine, but could be painful and dangerous unless very carefully used. (Children should be warned that leaves and berries are bad, and that spurges have nasty burning latex in the stems.) Caper Spurge is also sometimes recommended for deterring moles, which seems to be quite unfounded as far as the animals are concerned, and may always have been a 'Chinese whisper' relating to the use of spurge latex to burn off warts (and therefore moles on the skin?). Please do not do this at home either! Apart from this unfairly shaky reputation, this is a wonderful plant, with striking presence and architectural quality. Grigson (1958) calls it 'a garden treasure, a plant noble and curious in form', with 'aesthetic claims to replace its discarded medicinal virtues'. William Robinson (1870) said that its 'stately' appearance made it worthy of a place in a wild garden at least. Walter Ingwersen (1952) liked it 'to seed itself about in my garden for its stately carriage and strange beauty', and he also noted: 'It just seeds sufficiently to maintain itself, and nearly always comes in places requiring an exclamation mark, as it were ...', and 'is so easily pulled out should it crop up in a wrong place'. It may germinate in autumn or spring, and can reach nearly a metre in good growth. The leaves are a very dark green, striking in growth and unmistakable as seedlings.

Euphorbia serratula, correctly called Upright Spurge but always affectionately known as Tintern Spurge by botanists who have seen it at home in the Wye Valley, is now extremely rare as a wild plant. It seems to have been an introduction which never became widely established, was always restricted to deciduous limestone woodland in a few areas of England, and over the last century has declined even

Designer leaves – Caper Spurge always looks distinguished.

more, because it is in a conservation category of plants which are 'management dependent'. The woods where it grew produced some choice timbers, and were formerly managed, with open rides and tracks, and clearings when trees were felled. This kind of disturbance suited an annual/biennial lifestyle, as plants could grow fast when conditions were good, and seed would have been moved round. This also makes it an excellent garden plant, because bare soil and reasonable light are what it loves. It usually germinates in autumn, and does not mind being moved

Tintern Spurge on a forestry track – garden plants are taller and develop an airy, branching habit.

while it is small. The new leaf rosettes are rather ordinary, but are a pleasant green and can be planted close together to cover ground under shrubs. It is in flower that the Tintern Spurge is a treasure. Plants vary in size, but may reach 60cm, and the flowers are carried in profusion on very thin stalks. When a flowering stem is fully expanded the effect is like sprays of golden-green *Gypsophila*, airy and extremely pretty, contrasting with and enhancing surrounding leaf shapes and colours. This species will grow in sun or semi-shade, and more exposed plants often develop dashing red stem colour. Plants are good in shrubberies and shade beds, and in mixed border plantings. Seed is not widely available, but once established in a garden it will usually persist for years without ever being a nuisance.

Geranium pratense (Meadow Cranesbill); *G. robertianum* (Herb-Robert); *G. sanguineum* (Bloody Cranesbill); *G. sylvaticum* (Wood Cranesbill)

GERANIACEAE *(Cranesbill family)*

County flower of Northumberland: Bloody Cranesbill; Sheffield: Wood Cranesbill

Most gardeners are devoted to this genus, and a large number of species and cultivars are widely grown. Some have been in gardens for many years, and have had time to escape and become naturalized. These include *G. endressii* (French Cranesbill), *G. phaeum* (Dusky Cranesbill), *G. pyrenaicum* (Hedgerow Cranesbill) and *G. versicolor* (Pencilled Cranesbill). All these can have long-established populations in woods and on hedge banks, and may be locally valued as wild flowers. There is only room here to consider four of our real natives, but the family and genus are frequently mentioned in garden literature. Most of the related plants are distinctive because of the 'likeness of the unripe seed vessels to the head and beak' of certain birds (Bowles, 1914). The name Geranium comes originally from Greek *geranos* (a crane), *erodium* (storks' bills) from *erodios* (a heron), and *pelargonium* (geranium) from *pelargos* (a stork). Even with a bit of a mix-up between the birders and the botanists, several centuries ago, these names are clearly based on the unmistakable pods.

Meadow Cranesbill is familiar from many road verges, where occasional mowing suits it well. A plant of meadows and calcareous grassland, it is easy to grow as a garden plant, either in grass or in the border. Christopher Lloyd (2000) noted: 'It is easily raised from seed, which is the way my mother originally introduced it to our meadow' (at Great Dixter). He also remarked 'When the grass is cut [it] is the first plant to bounce back with new leaves and it sometimes flowers a second time' (which explains its long flowering season on road verges). Cranesbill leaves,

LEFT: 'Bird's-head' seed pods are characteristic of Cranesbills – this is Meadow Cranesbill. BELOW: The Somerset name 'Blue Basins' describes the flowers of Meadow Cranesbill.

in particular those of this species, are beautiful and it is worth the effort of cutting out shabby ones to encourage fresh growth. Flowers are generously produced and even if they fall quickly the buds keep coming. E.A. Bowles (1914) grew it 'almost too plentifully' on a rough bank where the 'crowd of blue blossoms is delightful in July' and he particularly enjoyed 'the long line of blue snow that lies on the path under them... till the next day's sun withers the fallen petals'. There are plenty of good garden selections in various colours. Whites and pinks are sometimes rather dingy, so try to see them in flower or choose a well-known variety. Among the best are 'Mrs Kendall Clark' with petals washed in subtle blues and greys, and the double 'Plenum Violaceum' with tight posy flowers of intense rich purple – both of these have the AGM. 'Bittersweet' is less widely available, but has really stylish dark anthers contrasting with almost white petals. All the Meadow Cranesbills like good soil, and although they need light and sun, they should not be allowed to get extremely dry. If plants in your garden grow large, put a corral of twigs round to support them. The flowering stems can flop if they are not in a close-growing meadow, and the fragile petals can get bedraggled.

Wood Cranesbill – beautiful but rather fleeting.

Bloody Cranesbill will flower all summer long, and more.

G. sylvaticum (Wood Cranesbill) looks as if it should be a wonderful addition to flower borders or to wilder parts of the garden but it is much less easy to grow than *G. pratense*. In spite of its name it is not a woodlander. It will take part-shade, not too deep, but is really a plant of continental alpine meadows or spray-watered Icelandic river gorges, where it flowers in spectacular profusion. In Britain it grows only in the north and in Scotland, and the key word for conditions where it will grow well is *cool*. It can be seen wild on damp road verges and grassy stream banks, and is a beautiful plant with shapely leaves of purest bright green and flowers in a range of purplish- blue shades,

some quite intense. If you can establish it in a shrubbery or in damp grassland it will look lovely in May, but has quite a brief flowering season, and does take real care and attention if you live further south than about York. This dependence on cool, moist conditions makes it less popular than *G. pratense*, but there are some very pretty named selections. 'Mayflower' (which has the AGM) and 'Amy Doncaster' are both good blues with an obvious white eye, and *G. sylvaticum* f. *roseum* 'Baker's Pink' is a delicious colour.

G. sanguineum really is an excellent garden plant. Its natural habitat is among calcareous rocks, most famously on the karst limestone of the Burren in Ireland and in the Derbyshire Dales, and occasionally on dunes where shell sand adds lime. The only unsatisfactory thing is the name, as the flower colour is brilliant magenta with no blood tones at all. Its habit is quite different from the taller meadow and wood cranesbills, as it spreads from a low central clump and flowers quite close to the ground, making it ideal for rockeries, paving and path edges. It flowers for much of the year, and indeed its only real fault is that it can creep too much, and its roots are very tough.

Robert Gathorne-Hardy (1961) who thought it one of the 'noblest' of our wild flowers, does admit that 'it must be more than twenty years since I began my unending war in the rock-garden against this magnificent barbarian', and unless you want it to develop a dazzling monoculture, it is best not to let it get in among immovable rocks or paving stones. In an ordinary border or gravel bed it can more easily be kept within bounds, and the months of colour are most rewarding. There are many colour forms and named selections available. The best known was found, reportedly on Walney Island, in the eighteenth century, and was formerly therefore called var. *lancastrense* (now var. *striatum*). It is a beautiful pearly pink, with slightly darker veins. Some gardeners are devoted to the pure white 'Album' AGM, which is slightly less compact, with taller, more slender flower stems. Others prefer some of the many excellent variations on the basic magenta. 'Shepherd's Warning' AGM is a very neat and charming form in a reddish pink without any 'puce' tone, while breeders are introducing delightful plants such as the hybrid 'Elke', which is a soft mauve-pink with a silver line round the petals.

G. robertianum (Herb-Robert) is one of the commonest wild flowers in Britain and Ireland. Its little pink flowers and straggly reddish stems can be seen in north and south, in town and country. Grigson (1958) collected more than a hundred local names for it, many connected with mischievous (or even malign) goblins and spirits such as Robin Goodfellow rather than any saintly figure, and it has never been an important garden plant like any of the preceding species. There is, however, one charming form, available from specialist seed lists as 'Celtic White' ('Album' is just a pallid form of the ordinary plant). Walter Ingwersen (1951) described it as 'a miniature Herb-Robert with finely cut, fern-like leaves in more or less rosette formation and a very prolonged display of white starry flowers'. The white is very pure, and the leaves and stems are intensely green with no trace of red or pink. He continues, 'I love to see this sowing itself prettily between mossy rocks and small ferns in cool corners, and have never found it in the least troublesome over a period of twenty years'. If you decide

Pure leaf and flower colours of 'Celtic White' contrast with ordinary Herb-Robert, which is infused with reds and pinks.

to introduce select self-seeders to your garden, this is one of the most modest and delightful, and will often attract approving comments.

Glaucium flavum (Yellow Horned-poppy)

PAPAVERACEAE *(Poppy family)*

Scattered around the coasts of England and Wales, rarer in Ireland and Scotland, this plant has an unforgettably dramatic appearance. It usually grows on shingle, occasionally on sand, and can form large, grand plants with the huge curved seed pods (the 'horns') reaching out beyond the grey leaves. The yellow petals have the slightly crumpled look shared by other poppies, and appear frail and papery, but like all strand-line specialists, this is a very tough plant. Because its immediate habitat may be damaged by winter storms (sand and shingle bars can easily be moved and reshaped by wave action) the strategy of the Yellow Horned-poppy is to be short-lived but produce plenty of salt-resistant seed. It takes easily to garden conditions, given enough light and sharp

The dramatic form of the Yellow Horned-poppy on a Dorset beach.

Iris pseudacorus (Yellow Iris, Yellow Flag)

IRIDACEAE *(Iris family)*

County flower of Wigtownshire

Britain and Ireland have only two native irises, and *I. foetidissima* (Stinking Iris or Gladdon) does not add to the summer garden because the flowers are a dingy colour and the leaves are inclined to spotted rust. It is recommended for autumn, having superb orange 'berries', and will be found in that chapter. The Yellow Iris, however, is an excellent species for summer use, because as well as the pond edges, river banks, bogs and ditches where it grows so lavishly in the country-side, it will tolerate much drier conditions in good garden soil. This is important, particularly in smaller gardens, because in wet ground the thick rhizomes can grow too strongly, and take over too much ground. They are also very tough to remove from, say, an overgrown pond. Drier ground restrains the plant, and slows down its spread, making some of the vari-eties and colour forms very desirable.

Hardly any of the 'garden' varieties are widely avail-able, though the easiest to find is also the most useful and reliable. This is 'Variegata' AGM, which has leaves with a broad creamy variegation which is really beau-tiful in fresh growth. The flowers are the ordinary yel-low, and by late summer the leaf colour will have become greener and duller, but in May this is a won-derfully effective plant for brightening and focusing plantings which have yet to develop. Other varieties need to be seen at close quarters, because their spe-cial appeal is in the flower, in particular in beautiful dark veining on the falls (the wide lower petals). The rich yellow 'Roy Davidson' AGM is an excellent exam-ple. Pale primrose selections include 'Crème de la Crème', but although double forms sound exciting they often have mean little flowers which don't open properly. There is also the curious hybrid 'Holden Clough' AGM, which may be the result of a chance meeting between the Yellow Iris (from damp habitat) and *I. chrysographes*, the 'Black' Iris (from drier habi-tats in China). The flowers are a strange mix of colours

drainage, and may behave as a biennial, or remain for two flowering summers. The number of seedlings produced varies between gardens, but the leaves are greyish from the first, so it is very easy to spot them and decide where you want them, and how many. Christopher Lloyd (2000) recommended finding a place for it (a gravel garden would of course be ideal) because 'the foliage is a feast in itself, highly glaucous and with wavy margins', and he was keen on the lovely f. *fulvum* with burnt orange petals. This is sometimes available from specialist nurseries or seed lists, and it is worth investing in a plant in flower if possible. This colour form seeds reasonably true, but there are usually some yellows in a batch, so it is worth starting with a 'seed packet' in the colour you want.

RIGHT: **Yellow Iris reflected in a Herefordshire pond.**
BELOW: *Iris pseudacorus* **'Variegata' AGM is stunning by a garden rill.**

(browns/blacks/yellows/greens), and not very large, but the plants are always well branched and flower for an astonishingly long time – there always seems to be one more bud to come. It is also useful for having a wide tolerance in growing conditions, having one 'wet' and one 'dry' parent. It will grow in both habitats, though of course sun is essential for good flowering. 'Holden Clough' is admittedly odd rather than conventionally beautiful, but its good nature and long flowering endear it to many. All these variant or related Yellow Flags, used as border plants rather than let loose in ponds, should show the good looks of the species without causing any problems. Yellow Iris is

also tall enough to be architectural, and planted in large clumps or along pond edge or stream, the handsome leaves can look great silhouetted against dark water or shrubs.

Jasione montana (Sheep's-bit)

CAMPANULACEAE *(Bellflower family)*

This plant with its little blue button flowers looks more like a diminutive scabious than a bellflower, and only close examination of one of the tiny florets reveals small botanical differences. It is very much one of the character plants of our western coasts, familiar on rocks and cliffs, or between the stones of Cornish hedges. As a wild plant it is associated with thin acid soils, though this seems to be more of a '*can do*' (in such poor habitats) than a '*must* do'. Walter Ingwersen (1951) grew it as a rockery plant, and observed that far from objecting to lime 'it seems to have no fads about soil and is easily grown and naturalized in not too stiff soils in any sunny spot'. Ingwersen founded a famous nursery specializing in rock plants, and he is one of the few garden writers to

Blue buttons – Sheep's-bit is modest but charming.

A touch of green – wild Narrow-leaved Everlasting Pea.

mention Sheep's-bit. 'It is little more than an annual but pretty enough for the outskirts of the rock garden, and I love to see it growing among heathers as it does so often in nature'. Its only real faults in garden terms seem to be its small size (rarely over 20cm) and short-lived plants (though left alone it will replace itself regularly), and perhaps its unfair reputation for tolerating only acid soils. Grown on a rockery, perhaps with Thrift or other familiar plants, it can be a very pretty and pleasant reminder of holidays and picnics. If you are a keen weeder and young plants seem hard to recognize, they have a very distinctive and rather fascinating smell when bruised.

Lathyrus sylvestris (Narrow-leaved Everlasting Pea)

FABACEAE, syn. PAPILIONACEAE
(Pea family), tribe 8 – FABEAE, syn. VICIEAE

The Everlasting Peas are not named for their flowers (though they do all have a good long season) but because of the very long persistence of their perennial root systems. Many *Lathyrus* species, both annual and perennial, are well known in gardens, in particular *L. odoratus* (Sweet Peas), but most of our natives are much less showy, and a number are quite uncommon. This modest climbing pea is scattered throughout most of Britain, growing in rough ground and scrub, along hedges or wood borders. It is very appealing to gardeners who like green in their flowers, because the buds are green with a maroon tinge, and the flowers open to old rose with green undertones. Foliage is narrow and bright green. Although too inconspicuous to grow as a specimen climber, there are many charming ways that it can be combined with other climbers, encouraged to scramble through hedging, or grown on low twiggy supports within herbaceous plantings. Keep the 'everlasting' bit in mind, and plant where it can remain undisturbed for a long time.

A bright denizen – *Lathyrus latifolius*.

An old favourite for garden fences –
Lathyrus grandiflorus.

A HELPING OF PEAS

Lathyrus sylvestris is the most garden-worthy of our native peas, but there are other delightful species (which may sometimes be available as seed) which can be grown in a wild garden or grass plot. They include: the common *L. pratensis* (Meadow Vetchling) with tufted yellow heads; the much less common *L. aphaca* (Yellow Vetchling) with singly held flowers; and the magical *L. nissolia* (Grass Vetchling) whose leaves are so like grass that it is almost impossible to spot until one of the exquisite little thread-stemmed vermilion flowers catches your eye.

L. linifolius (Bitter Vetch) is restricted to rather heathy acid soils, and can be grown in the same garden conditions as the popular Eastern European *L. vernus* (Spring Vetchling), which it rather resembles. A more spectacular (rare) native is the gorgeous *L. japonicus* (Sea Pea), but this is a highly specialized plant of maritime shingle bars, so needs special growing conditions.

Two garden escapes have also been widespread for years, persisting on roadsides, railway banks, in hedges near former gardens: *L. latifolius* (Broad-leaved Everlasting Pea) has unmistakable large puce racemes (there are excellent more restrained pink and white colour forms available to gardeners); and *L. grandiflorus* (Two-flowered Everlasting Pea), which is an old-fashioned beauty with a marvellous mix of purple tones in the flowers. Traditionally it was grown on garden fences.

Leucanthemum vulgare (Oxeye Daisy)

Oxeye Daisies in a surviving species-rich hay meadow.

ASTERACEAE, syn. COMPOSITAE *(Daisy family)*, subfamily 2 – ASTEROIDEAE, tribe 6 – ANTHEMIDEAE

Would you grow Oxeye Daisy in your garden? The answer may be 'yes', 'no', 'don't know', or all of these. This really is one of the most difficult of our wild flowers to recommend wholeheartedly, but it is also one of the most beautiful and easily grown, giving a guaranteed spectacular show every year, because it is a very vigorous plant with fast and efficient methods of increase. Growing on a Cornish cliff, Oxeye Daisy flowers with neat short stems look large for the size of plant, but this is because exposure to Atlantic gales dwarfs the stems, and the granite rocks of the cliffs only support thin poor soils with few

nutrients. In good garden soils the flower heads remain the same size, but the plant can grow up to a metre high – a giant in comparison. In the hay meadow pictured, the flowers are quite tall, and there are enough to make it a lovely sight, but even here there are pressures that make the plants work hard to produce such abundance. They are fighting for resources within a crowd including grasses (the little flower heads of *Briza media*, Quaking Grass, are visible in abundance), which can be the most competitive of all plants. Oxeye Daisies are tough and adaptable plants, aggressively competitive if given the chance.

In gardens they can become a pest, spreading by seed and root with astonishing speed, so they do need careful management. They can be lovely in grass that is allowed to grow after bulbs have flowered, perhaps on a rough bank with poor soil or in an unmown orchard, but they can only be allowed free rein where they are not within seeding range of open soil. Since about 2000 a few selections have appeared on the market, including 'Filigran' and 'Maikönigin' (May Queen), but they are not significantly different from the native species although they are merrily sold for general garden use. In 2007 Chicago Botanic Garden published the results of an evaluation trial of the larger *L. × superbum* (Shasta Daisy) cultivars of gardens, in which they had included the named Oxeye Daisy selections. These were praised for their reliable performance and early flowering, but only 'cautiously recommended because of rhizomatous habits and prolific seed production'.

Malva sylvestris (Common Mallow); *Malva moschata* (Musk-mallow)

MALVACEAE *(Mallow family)*

Mallows, and other members of this family (which includes *Abutilon*, *Hibiscus* and *Lavatera*) are extremely popular garden plants, but Britain and Ireland have very few native species. The most familiar of them, *M. sylvestris* (Common Mallow) is also an extremely

troublesome weed that is widespread and abundant in farmyards, on waste ground, and on disturbed road verges. It often appears in the unmade gardens around new houses, because it has an efficient 'seed-bank' and can germinate in former sites whenever the ground is disturbed. It grows fast, and can easily reach 1m if it has the chance, is perennial, and has extremely long, tough roots – so it is very unwelcome as a garden weed. However, it does have an occasional colour variant, which makes all the difference. The flowers are usually a rather disagreeable faded puce, but early in the twentieth century a blue form was reportedly found near the beach in Paignton, Devon. This flower sweeps away prejudice on sight, being a soft greyish-blue with indigo veins. The founder of Paignton Zoo, Herbert Whitley, was also a keen plantsman who ran a 'Botanic Nursery' at his home, Primley House. He was enchanted by this find, and propagated the mallow for sale, calling it 'Primley Blue'. It is still popular and widely available (with a number of more recent colour selections), but like many variants of wild plants it is not as tough as the original species. Growing well, it makes a perfect border plant with fresh green leaves and a very long flowering season, but it does need moisture-retentive soil. If plants get too dry, they may become covered with a bright orange rust, which ruins the foliage and can seriously weaken the plant as well as being very unsightly. Growing in good soil that does not dry out, and perhaps adding a compost mulch, should protect them.

Malva sylvestris **colour forms: (left) 'Primley Blue'; (above) 'Braveheart'.**

A stand of Musk-mallow on a roadside bank.

Musk-mallow, however, is very easy to recommend, and is already a denizen of many established gardens. It is a meadow and open grassland plant, often seen on sunny road banks, and the normal wild form has soft pink flowers. White flowers are also quite frequent, and are the colour most often introduced into gardens. Everything about this plant is pretty, because the leaves are very deeply divided giving an almost parsley-like effect. It will flower on and off all summer, coming again in autumn if cut back, and can be grown in any good soil as a border plant or in grass that is cut occasionally. There has to be a drawback though, and of course for some gardeners this will be its enthusiastic seeding habits! Seedlings are easy to recognize, though, as soon as they get their second leaves (which begin to show the divisions), and usually appear quite close to the perennial parent plant. Baby plants are easy to pot up for local plant sales and the white form in particular is popular.

Melittis melissophyllum (Bastard Balm)

LAMIACEAE, syn. LABIATAE
(Dead-nettle family)

This is really rather a rare plant, found only occasionally on wood edges, in scrub or on hedge banks in southwest Wales, across southwest England and as far as Hampshire. Most plants included in this book are more widespread and easier to find so that they can be seen 'at home', but this is a real treasure as a garden plant, and is quite widely available from specialist nurseries. There is also nothing rare or difficult about its habitat, and it will grow in any soil containing a reasonable amount of leaf mould, planted in semi-shade where it will not get too dry. This is a plant that deserves the effort of learning its Latin name (it's the only *Melittis* native or naturalized in England, so the genus name alone will do), since 'Bastard Balm' is both unattractive and uninformative. As Grigson (1958) wrote, this name 'sadly and badly distinguishes this much more handsome plant from the Balm, Bee Balm, or Balm Gentle of the gardens'. These are all names for *Melissa officinalis*, also known as Lemon Balm, which is invasive and often naturalized, but not native. Except for its golden or variegated forms in fresh leaf, it is also rather a scruffy plant, while the *Melittis* is dignified and shapely in all stages of growth, and has large beautiful flowers. In the wild form, these are white with a broad dark pink lip, but there are also a number of garden selections including white, all-pink, and bicolors with lips in various shades of paler or darker pinks and mauves. This is a lovely and unusual plant, quite as exotic as *Lamium orvala*, the large dead nettle from central Europe which has been fashionable since the middle of the last century. *Melittis* produces upright stems to 70cm, and flowers in summer, so can add great interest to shrubbery plantings when spring blossom is over. Some sun suits it, and moisture retentive soil is important – this is definitely not a plant for dry, deep shade.

Myrrhis odorata (Sweet Cicely)

APIACEAE, syn. UMBELLIFERAE (Carrot family))

This handsome 'umbel' may have been introduced to gardens in medieval times as a medicinal and culinary herb. It was certainly familiar to Tudor gardeners and herbalists, and was used for flavouring and as a tonic. All its parts – roots, leaves and particularly the seeds and seed pods are aromatic and edible. It was not recorded in the wild till nearly the end of the eighteenth century, and is classed as a 'neophyte', but has become very well established in northern parts of England and Wales, in much of Scotland, and in parts of Northern Ireland. It can grow very abundantly on roadsides and river banks, often with more distinguished natives such as *Campanula latifolia* (Giant Bellflower) or *Cirsium heterophyllum* (Melancholy Thistle). Botanists from southern counties watch for these and for the first Sweet Cicely on a road verge to tell them that they are reaching the north and its special flora. There are not many local names recorded (another sign that it has not been here for many centuries), and 'Sweet Cicely' is a pretty name, but actually rather bland and generic. 'Sweet' must refer to the taste (though piling the leaves into jam to sweeten it, as advised during the 1970s' craze for wild food, is a signal failure); 'Cicely' as well as being a girls' name, may echo 'seseli', which is still the name of a genus and was formerly used for several groups in the same family.

Seen growing vigorously in almost natural habitat, Sweet Cicely is strikingly handsome. The leaves are well cut, almost fern-like, and the strong upright stems can easily reach a metre tall. Flowers are white, similar to those of many Cow Parsley relatives, but the seed cases, when still green, give a most interesting effect. They are held in upright clusters and are shaped rather like spectacle cases, wider at the top end.

All parts of the plant taste of anise or liquorice, but these green pods and seeds have the best flavour, and can be added raw to salads and sandwich fillings or

Green on green – the leaves and seed pods of Sweet Cicely are lovely.

scattered on soups or vegetables. In the garden it is usually recommended for the herb garden or potager only, though a few writers such as Ingwersen (1951) who grew it 'for its finely cut and lacy foliage and for the sweet and aromatic taste of its seeds', noted that 'any common border treatment suits it'. Other authorities give a caution regarding its deep roots and ability to seed lavishly, and several find the flowers dull, but there may be other reasons why it should be so unfashionable. Its northern distribution may give a clue, because like Wood Cranesbill it needs cool conditions and dislikes being too dry. Part shade and

Bistort with Wood Cranesbill in the French Alps – such abundance would be unlikely in modern Britain.

deep soil in a herb or vegetable garden could suit, but border conditions might be too hot and dry. Another reason may be subjective, 'in the eye of the beholder', because some plants that look terrific as wild flowers may lose some of their charm in the garden. Even if they do not become a pest, or grow far too big and fall flat, they may lose an indefinable focus, and just look rather ordinary. Your taste buds and cooking habits are probably what matter most when you are deciding whether to grow this plant.

Persicaria bistorta, syn. *Polygonum bistorta* (Common Bistort)

POLYGONACEAE *(Knotweed family)*

Docks and knotweeds, even some sorrels, are generally unpopular. Both farmers and gardeners know them as annoying weeds, and they are usually perceived as ugly. Even their botanical names can be troublesome because '*Polygonum*' and '*Persicaria*' seem to play musical chairs, change and change about, so it is good to keep in mind that the names may vary but the plants themselves remain the same. Normally, Latin names make it clear which plant is being discussed, but in this family English names may sometimes be more consistent. Common Bistort is in the same genus as the very common (and despised) Redshank and Water-pepper, but is perennial and much more handsome and substantial than these straggling annual weeds. This is a native plant, and a benign one, with plenty of history. The name 'Bistort' may refer back to Latin ('twice-turned') because of its twisted roots, and it also has the local name 'Snake-weed' from the same feature, but in the north of England, the heartland of its distribution, it is more often known as 'Easter Ledges' or some variation of 'Easter Mangiants'. These names now sound impossibly arcane, but are actually perfectly sensible. 'Easter Ledges' (or 'Easter Ledger') was the name of a pudding eaten in the last weeks of Lent, and which was believed to help conception. 'Easter Mangiants' is another name for the same dish. 'Mangiants' ('magiants', 'mentgions', and so on) just means Easter food, coming from the French *manger*, to eat. The pudding, a savoury mix to accompany meat dishes when Lent is over, or more abstemiously on its own, is still made in parts of northern England, and can be used as a general spring pick-me-up in the style of other cleansing greens such as Nettles or Dandelions.

In flower in May and June, this plant is extremely pretty as a mass of clear pink heads like miniature bottle brushes, but it is seldom seen in quantity in Britain now because its favourite habitat of damp unimproved meadows has greatly declined. The photograph is taken in the French Alps, and shows how our northern fields could once have looked. Even a much smaller patch is a delight to find (the leaves are also attractive, a classic dark green 'leaf shape').

Because of its historic popularity as a tonic it occurs as a garden escape throughout Britain. This is an excellent plant for a pond edge, the side of a rill, or damp grassland. The cultivated selections such as the large-flowered 'Superba' AGM, or the much darker pink subsp. *carnea*, can also be grown as border flowers, but they really do need to be in moisture-retentive soil. They are long-lived, spreading a bit but not furiously, and flower for months, so if you can establish Bistort with perhaps Siberian Irises (even with *Meconopsis* blue poppies if you live in Scotland!), with pink and blue *Aquilegia* or with a colour range of

Neat and nice – Mouse-ear Hawkweed.

Astilbe, and leave them to their own devices in a damp area of your garden, this will give a lovely and low-maintenance mix.

Pilosella aurantiaca (Fox-and-cubs); *P. officinarum* (Mouse-ear Hawkweed)

ASTERACEAE, syn. COMPOSITAE *(Daisy family)*, tribe 2 – LACTUCEAE, syn. CICHORIEAE

Fox-and-cubs is native to central and northern Europe, and is merely a naturalized garden escape in Britain. Mouse-ear Hawkweed is native, but is an inconspicuous little creeping perennial, spreading by means of thin stolons, impossible to grow as a specimen plant, and too straggly for rockery use. So why is either species included here? The answer involves a subject that really divides gardeners, whether they are wildflower-minded or not – flowery lawns! Lawns originally enclosed from fields sometimes still have native flowers as part of the turf (if years of chemical treatment applied to yield the desired 'green velvet' have not removed them all), and some modern gardeners appreciate such relics, or are prepared to add

Fox-and-cubs opens its russet flowers in sunlight.

will flower all summer, and a group is extremely pretty because of the multiple flower heads of such an unusual colour. Like many members of this family, the flowers open in sun and close in rain or dull weather. In this case the foxy colour becomes hidden in hairy sepals which are almost black. Because of its height it is best for longer grass that is less often mown, or for grassy banks supporting only thin vegetation. Poor soil is fine for this plant once it is established, and it will both creep and seed. It is occasionally seen as a welcome denizen in nurseries, though it needs to be removed from pots and containers before it squeezes out the rightful inhabitant.

Plantago major (Greater Plantain); *P. media* (Hoary Plantain)

PLANTAGINACEAE *(Plantain family)*

Robert Gathorne-Hardy in his book *The Native Garden* (1961) begins a section: 'We don't as a rule think of Plantains as ornamental... when we find them in the garden, we get rid of every one as quickly as we can', but he goes on to describe a fascinating freak form which is occasionally produced by both the Greater and Hoary Plantain. The flower spike becomes a head with little leaves instead of flowers, so the plants sometimes have really decorative green heads. A form of this kind is known as a 'Rose Plantain', the same gardener noting that 'in the better forms the head is flat, so that the flower looks indeed like a little green [double] Rose' (though in others misshapen leaflets cling to the usual spike, looking far less attractive). E.A. Bowles (1914) describes growing a 'rose' form from each species in his collection of oddities – he had a corner of his garden he called 'The Lunatic Asylum' – and he particularly valued them for their long history in gardens. Tudor gardeners and nurserymen were intrigued by the development of these curious 'flowers', and collected and enjoyed the well-shaped ones as garden plants. If you can source a good form, it makes a delightful oddity and actually looks very

some flowers of their own. It is a subject that raises strong feelings, but a few plants have been included in this book for those who wish to consider them.

Mouse-ear Hawkweed is a plant of thin short grass, often sheep-nibbled and in dry sunny places. A lawn is perfect habitat for it, particularly along the edges where the stolons can explore into the path. In suitable conditions the plantlets grow close together, their hairy leaves hugging the ground, single lemon-yellow hawkweed flowers held above on short silvery stalks. If you enjoy daisies and more in your lawn, this is a good addition, flowering between each cut, and with such flat leaves that they are seldom damaged.

Fox-and-cubs is a taller plant, the flower stalks (up to 25cm) holding a cluster of truly fox-russet heads. It

Hoary Plantain flower with a Small Heath Butterfly.

handsome thing when well grown [with] leaves as red as those of a Beetroot', but it does behave just like its weedy sibling, and seeds profusely, so introducing it to your garden needs to be an informed decision. Seedlings are reddish from the start, so are easy to weed out, and a developed plant growing in good light and sun can be a glorious colour, though it may take some effort to keep plants where you want them to be. Grown close to a path, it's very possible to dead-head. This plant likes open, disturbed ground, and needs sunlight to develop good colour. It is not possible to grow it among grass.

Hoary Plantain does grow in grassy habitats, in grazed turfs with good light. It is included here because of its potential as a plant for flowery lawns, having both delightful catkin-like pale mauve flower heads, and flat sculptural leaf rosettes, which stay below the level of a mower blade. It can be started from plug plants or seeds, and should be available from nurseries that produce native plants for calcareous meadow projects. The abundant pollen produced is good for bees and other insects, and the ridged leaf blades have a slight shine that highlights their shape beautifully. Single plants introduced into a lawn will increase slowly by additional rosettes, eventually forming a close-knit patch.

well with other green shades and leaf textures, but of course it cannot seed, and is not the kind of plant to make any fortunes by micro-propagation, so it is now rare in gardens. The RHS *Plant Finder* usually lists some specialist nurseries that stock *P. major* 'Rosularis' (formerly called 'Bowles' Variety'). The Greater Plantain does, however, produce another much more widely available garden variety, the Red-leaved Plantain *P. major* 'Rubrifolia'. Bowles describes this as 'a

Sculpture at lawn-level – Hoary Plantain leaf rosettes.

Detail of Meadow Clary flowers.

Salvia pratensis (Meadow Clary); *S. verbenaca* (Wild Clary)

LAMIACEAE, syn. LABIATAE – *(Dead-nettle family)*

The tall blue flower spikes of Meadow Clary are unquestionably grand and beautiful enough to hold their own among garden plants, and are reasonably easy to grow in most warm, well-drained garden soils, though its wild sites are always calcareous. It is,

however, considerably rarer than most of the plants recommended in this book, and is at the centre of many conservation efforts (including Plantlife's 'Back from the Brink' programme). Native sites are few, scattered thinly across southern England usually in unimproved chalk grassland, and some have been recorded in the same place for considerable lengths of time, even since the seventeenth century. The species never seems to have been common though, and now can be seen only in nature reserves. It certainly deserves a place in any sunny garden both for its beauty and to honour its position as one of the flagship species of current plant conservation. It is reasonably easy to find on nursery lists, with about twelve selections available. Colour forms include various blues, pink and white. The 'Haematodes' group and the dark blue 'Indigo' have been awarded AGMs, and some of the varieties in the modern 'Ballet' series are gaining a reputation for good looks.

Wild Clary is much more widespread, occurring in much of Britain, though rarer in Ireland and Scotland. It also is a calcicole, but can be seen in quite scruffy places as well as in pristine grassland. Seaside car parks or downland view-points are possible sites, because the nice flat dark rosettes of crinkled basal leaves are very sturdy, and can be walked or driven

Meadow Clary in a superb meadow community, with Pyramidal Orchid, Oxeye Daisy, Quaking Grass and Sorrel.

'A touch of eye-liner' – Wild Clary.

over without destroying the plant. This species flowers freely during a long season, and although the flowers are small, the dark hairs on stems, leaves and calyces give it quite a smart appearance (like a touch of eye-liner).

Grigson (1958) thought the plant 'rather fascinating' and called the stems 'blue-dyed'. Brought into the garden, it is another candidate for flowery lawn or grass plot treatments, and to grow among pale soft-looking grasses such as *Stipa tenuissima*. In flower-bed conditions it may seed too freely, and is fond of getting into gravel paths, so is best planted first where it can spread if it wants. Like most sages (the *Salvia* genus), it was once used as a beneficial herb, though a popular way of treating eye infections by sticking a soaked seed, swelled up like frog-spawn, into each eye, has thankfully gone out of fashion!

Sedum acre (Biting Stonecrop), section 5 – *Sedum*; *S. anglicum* (English Stonecrop), section 5 – *Sedum*; *S. dasyphyllum* (Thick-leaved Stonecrop), section 5 – *Sedum*; *S. rosea* (Roseroot), section 1 – *Rhodiola*; *S. telephium* (Orpine), section 3 – *Telephium*

CRASSULACEAE *(Stonecrop family)*

Christopher Lloyd, always outspoken, wrote in 2000: 'Sedums are something of a minefield, even excluding the rock-garden types. All are succulent and many do not fit easily into normal mixed borders. All require perfect drainage...', but having given this fair warning he goes on to acknowledge that they are 'ideally suited' to gravel gardens 'where they stand out as prima-donnas' (in the best sense – he was a great opera fan). He also mentions the value of the persistent flower heads on the taller species, changing colour but remaining handsome right into the winter. Four of our native species are noted below, some of which have close relatives that have escaped from gardens and become naturalized.

The largest section (*Sedum*) includes many little rock plants from cliffs, sand and shingle beaches and stony hills, which flourish in man-made habitats too and are mostly very familiar from ruins, stone walls and old roofs. Biting Stonecrop (also called 'Wall-pepper') is the one most often seen, and always considered a cheerful sight when its mass of shining yellow flowers is out.

It is nicely summed up by Walter Ingwersen (1951): '... in many country villages the roofs of most of the houses have larger or smaller patches growing upon them and decking them with splashes of golden yellow in the flowering season. A pretty enough little plant but to be used with care, as every fat little leaf that falls off is quite capable of growing into a new

Biting Stonecrop is golden in flower.

Stonecrop leaves are appealing – English Stonecrop on a Devon cliff, with leaves of Spring Squill.

plant...'. Modern property values may have led to clean rural house roofs, but it is still charming for walls and outhouses, and for use in 'green roof' projects. Even a bird table or small summerhouse can be used for such an experiment, and native stonecrops are ideal as they can establish their root-mats with almost no soil. Robert Gathorne-Hardy records his guilty pleasure as a child when he persuaded visitors who didn't know their plants that the little leaves tasted delicious, and then laughed 'horridly at their expression as the mouth started smarting like Nettle stings'. Biting Stonecrop or Wall-pepper is well named, being completely harmless, but fiercely 'hot'.

English Stonecrop is very common around the coasts of Ireland and west Britain, its pink-and-white flowers in the background of many holiday memories. Like Biting Stonecrop it forms little mats on very shallow soils, and can be used in paving stones, rockeries and gravel edges as well as being introduced to walls. Gathorne-Hardy used to recommend 'planting the two species together, so that the mingled colours enhance each other', but he admits that he never got around to actually trying this himself, so it could be a charming experiment for your garden!

Two rather similar species, *S. album* (White Stonecrop) and *S. dasyphyllum* (Thick-leaved Stone-crop), are garden escapes, established here and there in Britain and Ireland. White Stonecrop has upstanding

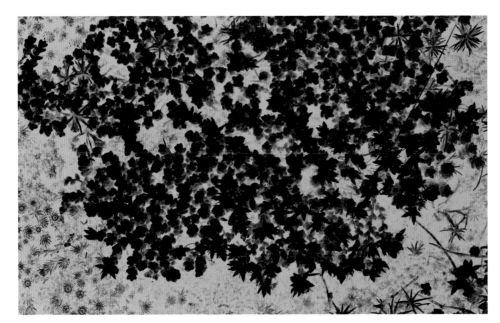

English Stonecrop flowers.

Unusual jade-and-rose colouring in Thick-leaved Stonecrop leaves.

flower stems to 25cm, rather than the flowers open-ing among the leaves. It can be pretty among paving or gravel, or particularly on wall tops. However, Thick-leaved Stonecrop, in spite of the clunky name, is more exotic than any of the previous species, and also much more rarely seen. Naturalized populations on walls or rock faces (for instance in road or rail cut-tings) seem to be very long-lasting, and are always valued by local botanists. The very fat little leaves are

dotted with tiny glands and often have reddish colouring, making them look like minute birds' eggs, and the whitish flowers are also stained with pink or wine tones. It is probably too succulent to be grown where it might be trodden on, but established on a rockery or mossy wall it is the most delightful oddity.

Roseroot is a startlingly different plant, and indeed has a startling appearance altogether. It is a plant of mountains and cliffs, producing substantial flower

LEFT: **Roseroot has architectural structure.**
BELOW: **Wild Orpine** is the origin of many good garden selections.

stems up to 35cm tall, growing from a comparatively massive branched tuberous rhizome. The flowers (a dull yellow) and mature leaves are not particularly outstanding among the many tall garden stonecrops available, though grand-looking high on a rock ledge. The real fascination of the plant is when the leaf rosettes start to appear from the rhizome (everything dies down in the autumn, so the winter rhizome just looks like a knotted miniature tree stump). Gathorne-Hardy loved the stage in spring when the leaves first start to unfold, and the plant 'puts one in mind of some magical, monstrous piece of architectural carving carried out in opaque crystal'. Ingwersen recommends finding room 'for a plant or two in a wall or on rocks with only a minimum of earth' – the big roots may rot in soft soil. He also notes that in northern England, Scotland and Ireland, 'cottagers grow it in pots as a window plant', and this may still be good management, using really stony compost and making sure that the pot is on the *outside* of any window. The name comes from a surprising quality – the roots really are scented. Gerard (1597) said that they smell 'like the damaske Rose', and they can be sliced and dried for adding to pot-pourri.

Low-growing 'Herbstfreude' AGM (formerly 'Autumn Joy') looks good flowering amongst *Euphorbia cyparissias* **'Fen's Ruby'.**

The last in the list of recommended native stonecrops is also the most important. *S. telephium* (Orpine) was valued in folk medicine for centuries. It is harmless, and rather as people now who have aloes as house plants use a broken leaf to rub on small burns, the succulent Orpine leaves were used to soothe cuts. Grigson (1958) refers to it as a 'cottage vulnerary', but he also lists more exciting uses because it used to be thrown on the great bonfires on St John's Eve (the night before Midsummer), and used in many ways for divination by girls wanting to find out about their future love lives. Nowadays, it is more importantly used for predicting popular and fashionable garden plants! The wild plant often has rather dingy pinkish flowers, though more purple

forms can turn up. It grows on banks and woodland edges, sometimes forming large populations that persist for years unless the habitat is destroyed.

Various good colour forms have been collected by gardeners in the past, and more recently there has been much work selecting and interbreeding within the group, producing a lovely range of both leaf and flower colours ranging from strong beetroot reds to subtle fruit fool colours with tinges of green and cream. There is also a range of habit, from tall, upright plants to some that are almost prostrate. The *Plant Finder* list usually has around thirty-five named varieties, groups and subspecies, including the wonderful 'Purple Emperor', which has gained an AGM. Orpine has been much used in hybridization as well, and very popular sedums such as 'Matrona' AGM, and 'Herbstfreude' AGM (formerly 'Autumn Joy') have Orpine 'blood'. Sedums, usually in the form of *S. spectabile* (the 'Ice-plant' of 1950s' gardens), are frequently recommended to attract butterflies, which indeed they do, but they also attract a large variety of bees and other late summer flying insects, so cross-pollination between cultivars is common. If you don't mind waiting to see how seedlings turn out, this can yield treasures. Indeed, a terrific effect can develop in gravel or on a dry bank where the compatible plants cross and scatter young until a range of leaf and flower colours create a whole new palette.

Another two stonecrops are sometimes seen established on walls, cliffs or banks. Both are suitable for walls and rockeries, but they are very difficult to tell apart. *S. forsterianum* (Rock Stonecrop) is actually a very rare native with scattered sites in Wales and southwest England, but as it is quite a frequent garden plant its status can be hard to assess. *S. rupestre* (formerly *S. reflexum*) Reflexed Stonecrop, is not native but sometimes becomes naturalized. Both have pleasant reddish leaf colouring if grown in good light, and leafy flowering stems up to 25cm or so with pretty clustered yellow flowers at the top.

Stachys officinalis, syn.* *Betonica officinalis* (Betony)

LAMIACEAE, syn. LABIATAE
(Dead-nettle family)

In Britain and Ireland plants in the *Stachys* genus are usually referred to as 'woundworts', herbs used for healing cuts. Betony for a very long time was the most important of this group, highly valued by the ancient Greeks and Romans and then throughout medieval Europe. It was believed to cure many illnesses and heal all wounds, and was implicated in magical and mythological lore (Chiron the centaur, half man, half horse, was supposed by some to have discovered the herb). It was believed to be a protection against witchcraft and 'elf sickness', though by 1669 Culpeper was more prosaically recommending it for the domestic medicine cupboard 'in Syrup, Conserve, Oyl, Oyntment, and Plaister'. Unfortunately, as Grigson (1958) noted, 'Betony is a fraud, with no out-

Betony in grass heath with *Erica cinerea* **(Bell Heather).**

standing virtue of any kind', and in more recent garden history it has rather slipped between two stools. It is known to have no medicinal value, but garden writers dismiss it as 'of more interest to the herbalist than the gardener' (Ingwersen 1951). It is actually an attractive plant, found in unimproved damp grasslands and grass heath throughout much of Britain, but much rarer in Ireland. It is suitable for rather acid soils, and in the garden can be grown with summer-flowering heathers.

Harebells make a very pretty planting companion, with Sheep's-bit for the front edge. The normal wild colour is quite a strong magenta-purple, but if you prefer gentler colours there are now several selections available, in white or a range of pinks, including 'Rosea Superba'. A continental selection called 'Hummelo' has large purple heads on strong stems, and is free-flowering, but perhaps the choicest variety is a rather dwarf white. This has short flower stems, often less than 20cm, and the leaves make an enchanting little mat on the ground. These leaves have a bit of a shine and neatly scalloped edges, so grown in the front of a border, or in a raised bed or trough, the plants are delightful whether in flower or not.

Thalictrum flavum (Common Meadow-rue); T. minus (Lesser Meadow-rue)

RANUNCULACEAE (Buttercup family)

Neither of these plants is very common, but they are both delightful, so it could be worth the effort of consulting a local flora group, or the BSBI online *Atlas* to see if they grow near you. The splendidly tall Common Meadow-rue grows in fen country, along streams and ditch sides, so if you live near the Somerset Levels or the Norfolk Broads, you could be lucky. Lesser Meadow-rue occurs more unpredictably inland, but there is a seaside form (sometimes called subsp. *arenarium*), which may be seen in scrubby, grassy places on well-vegetated 'grey' sand dunes. The flowers of this plant are small and brown, quite unlike the yellow puffs of its taller relative, and what you are most likely to spot are the leaves. Walter Ingwersen (1951) praises its 'dainty fern-like foliage resembling Maidenhair and quite fit to associate with the smaller cut flowers in a specimen vase'.

They are both good garden plants, and Robert Gathorne-Hardy (1961) intelligently calls them 'catalysts', pointing out that in their different ways they will both 'enhance the beauty of neighbouring flowers'. He grew Lesser Meadow-rue with the pale form of Bloody Cranesbill, at first because they both came from Walney Island; later simply because they were so pretty together. It is a good rockery plant, or for edging a path, and will accept semi-shade. Common Meadow-rue (sadly now not common at all, but in decline everywhere due to habitat loss) is a much grander plant, often over 1m tall. Christopher Lloyd (2000) considered it an important June flower, 'with pouffes of pale yellow flowers above boldly glaucous foliage'. Ingwersen calls it 'a giant for the back of the border or ... in moist ground. This plant will easily reach 3 to 4 feet in height at the time it waves aloft its panicles of feathery, soft yellow flowers .... In it we have a first-rate garden plant.' As well as producing this tall display the leaves are beautiful as they unfold in May, with the grey bloom on them fresh and unmarked. Both these natives are quite widely avail-able from specialist nurseries. Look for *T. flavum* subsp. *glaucum* to get the best grey foliage, and there is a selection called 'Illuminator', which has the new foliage coming through primrose to pale gold in colour, though it darkens at flowering time. Try to buy this as a spring plant, making sure that you have the special variety. Common Meadow-rue really does need moist soil, though the smaller plant likes things drier.

Umbilicus rupestris (Navelwort, Pennywort)

CRASSULACEAE (Stonecrop family)

Pictured at the beginning of this chapter, in Tresco Abbey Gardens, this is a humble but effective little plant. It grows wild in rock crevices, on cliffs and in ravines, and settles easily into man-made habitats. There can hardly be an old wall or stone-faced bank in the West Country without some plants, and it is an easy and trouble-free garden denizen, sometimes giving charming chance effects. The flower spikes are creamy, sometimes reddening as they age in a sunny wall, and staying in place into the autumn. Although the appearance is never spectacular, a group flowering together, or a wall dotted with the smooth green 'pennies' with their navel-like central dimple, is always pleasing. Establishing plants in walls is never as easy as it appears – often roots stuffed in with some token compost die off almost immediately, because they need to reach into the cool crevices deep inside, where they will not get hot or dry. Sometimes a loose stone or brick can be removed for you to plant the roots in a solid earth plug, and then replaced gently, or the front of the gap secured with smaller stones. Plants can also be put in existing or custom-made hollows on the top of the wall, in the hope that they will gradually seed downwards. A perfect situation for Navelwort and plants such as Sheep's-bit and small ferns, is one of the stone-faced banks known as a 'Cornish hedge', because there is plenty of soil packed round the construction stones. Navelwort will grow in sun or shade, as long as the roots are tucked away, and can also be introduced to raised beds and rockeries.

Verbascum lychnitis (White Mullein); *V. nigrum* (Dark Mullein); *V. thapsus* (Great Mullein, Aaron's Rod)

SCHROPHULARIACEAE *(Figwort family)*

Every gardener knows what a splendid genus this is. Mulleins provide some of the grandest and most fascinatingly coloured of border plants, and during their short lives (as biennials or very short-lived perennials) both leaves and flowers are very effective. There are five species native to Britain and Ireland, but two of them are both rare and rather too coarse in appearance to recommend for the garden. *V. pulverulentum* (Hoary Mullein), very large and branched, is occasionally found on bare chalky soils in East Anglia; *V. virgatum* (Twiggy Mullein) is an uncommon plant of waste ground in Devon and Cornwall. A number of garden species have also become established in places; the best known are probably *V. blattaria* (Moth Mullein) and *V. chaixii* (Nettle-leaved Mullein), both of which have garden selections including attractive white forms.

Of the three recommended species, White Mullein is the most uncommon as a wild plant, scattered throughout southern England on bare or disturbed calcareous soils. It is very beautiful, growing up to 1.5m, with the whole plant (certainly while fresh) silvered with soft hairs. All the mulleins need sun, but can be grown as border plants, on open banks, or round the edges of shrubberies, wherever they are unshaded. This one can be grown with other tall mulleins, mixing it with yellow-flowered forms, or on its own to 'lift' the appearance of darker surrounding foliage. Flowers on a mullein spike are not all open at once, but keep developing for weeks. This alone makes them valuable, but it also makes white-flowered mulleins easier to place as the colour appears

Complementary colours – White Mullein and Great Mullein.

more silvery from a distance than pure white, and has a correspondingly gentler effect.

Dark Mullein is also a calcicole, found through much of central and southern Britain and central Ireland on banks and waste ground, often established for years on managed road verges. It is a smaller plant, usually growing in groups, with simple flower spikes and, as the name suggests, rather dark green leaves. Its real beauty is in the flowers, which are usu-

ABOVE: **Dark Mullein has spectacular anthers and filaments.**
RIGHT: **The tall 'rod' of Great Mullein among wild summer grasses.**

ally a rich yellow with spectacular fuzzy purple anther filaments. This species is best grown near the front of a border, among small shrubs, or ideally raised on a bank or bed so that the flowers are easily visible. The *Verbascum* genus grows easily from seed, and some species will keep a population going once it is established in your garden. Some germinate in autumn, so may flower in their first summer, or you can plan for their biennial routine as you do for foxgloves.

Great Mullein is a common wild plant that has always been closely associated with people. It has dozens of local names (Aaron's Rod is one of the commonest, being an Old Testament reference to a dry

stick that miraculously burst into flower) and many of them have candle associations, or are of the 'rabbits' ears' kind because of the softly furry leaves. Grigson (1958) quotes Henry Lyte, who described the plant in 1578: 'The whole toppe with its pleasant yellow floures sheweth like to a wax candle'. Another Tudor plantsman, Parkinson, says that dried stalks were 'dipped in suet to burne' – presumably a bundle could be lit like an Olympic torch. Like all the mulleins, this one grows well in disturbed ground, and is a typical plant of dry banks, quarry spoil and ruins. It grows and seeds freely in the garden, as long as you are not on acid soil, and is easy to manage

Strongly coloured Wood Vetch on a Scottish shingle bank. Less-exposed plants have paler flowers.

Vicia sylvatica (Wood Vetch)

FABACEAE, syn. PAPILIONACEAE – *(Pea family)*

because of the distinctive baby plants that are furry from the start. The very tall and simple flower stem means that it is best grown in company, because a single plant can look rather foolish on its own. The back of a sunny border is good, or an open bank.

The only problem it has is a moth whose caterpillars feed on mulleins (and occasionally buddleias and figworts). This is a dingy little noctuid moth called *Cucullia verbasci* whose caterpillars hatch around midsummer. They are beautiful creatures with black, yellow and blue markings on a pale grey ground which blends with the silvery mullein leaves, but they can make those leaves vanish like magic if you do not spot them in time and pick them off. If the mulleins have already given a good show, or if the leafy stems are hidden by other plants, you can be a wildlife benefactor and allow the stems to be stripped; otherwise be on your guard.

In general, vetches are a pest in the garden. They look frail with their thin trailing stems, but they are extremely invasive and have amazingly tough, wiry roots. The term 'tare', which is part of the name of several wild vetches, is associated with weediness, because they are plants which can harm crops by choking them, cancelling the beneficial effects gained from this family's ability to fix nitrogen in the soil. Some of the common British natives flourish among rough tall grasses and in the dense communities of hedge banks, where their ability to twine and climb brings success in these highly competitive habitats, but also makes them unwelcome garden denizens. Wood Vetch shares these vigorous qualities, but its beauty, and the fact that it will tolerate shade, means that it can be used to great advantage within gardens if carefully placed. It is quite a long-lived perennial, which also increases by seed and has a wide range of tolerance in matters of soil and light.

Wood Vetch produces long trailing stems that grow longer throughout the late spring and summer, until they die off in autumn after the seed pods ripen. In the wild this vetch can grow in surprising places, not just in rocky woodland or on shady banks but also in very exposed sites. In north Devon it grows lavishly on sea cliffs, and it is also known from both natural ravines and road or railway cuttings. This toughness gives it a wide range of garden uses, one of the best being to grow it (as some gardeners now grow small-flowered and species clematis) to cover banks and stumps, or just to ramble over rocky ground or rubble. It can also be persuaded to scramble near the foot of hedges and shrubs, though in the wild it favours reaching *down* rocks or banks rather than climbing strongly *upwards*. If you want to cover a bare bank, Wood Vetch should be planted near the top, encouraging a waterfall effect. The neat, pinnate leaves grow quite close, so a big plant can cover plenty of ground, and the flower spikes are also large (for a wild vetch). These look pale, almost white from a distance, but at close quarters the exquisite violet-purple veins show clearly. If you are a tidy gardener, old dead growth can be cleared off in early spring, but if you want to disguise the growing surface it is as well to leave the dry stems like netting to help new growth spread quickly. This species also makes a spectacular container plant if grown in a pot on top of a wall or pillar so the stalks fall like a curtain, and it can be placed in sun or shade so long as the roots can remain reasonably cool and moist. A layer of small stones on top of good earth-based potting compost is helpful.

Additional summer flowers for possible garden use

Annuals

Many of the plants associated with the 'wildflower gardening' fashion are annuals or biennials which probably grew as agricultural weeds in historic times. To grow them as a pretty mixture in the garden it is necessary to manage a plot as a miniature cornfield, 'ploughing' it in late summer, sowing the seed in autumn or spring, enjoying the flowers and then 'harvesting' (cutting back or raking off the dead stalks) before 'ploughing' again. If perennial weeds creep in the effect is ruined because the pretty annuals will not be able to compete, although they keep a secret weapon as their seeds are very long-lasting in the ground, ready to germinate for years to come when conditions are right. You may not want to model a garden bed on the old-fashioned farming year for long, but an all-annual sowing is very enjoyable as an occasional treat, and can be very useful for short-term colour as a quick fix for a newly dug bed, or to have something to enjoy while you concentrate on the inside of a new house. Most ready-mixed seed packets will include *Centaurea cyanus* (Cornflower) and *Agrostemma githago* (Corncockle). These are both 'archaeophytes' (ancient introductions by humans) and are now nearly extinct as wild plants though readily available from seed lists. They are pretty and would once have been common so are perfectly appropriate. All these 'weed' mixtures are most successful in poor soils, because without a crop to prop them up they grow too tall in good soils and flop terribly. Attractive species to try include the following:

Adonis annua (Pheasant's-eye)

An extremely beautiful buttercup relative with crimson, black-eyed flowers and feathery leaves. It needs sun and limy soils, and is rare now as a wild plant.

Pheasant's-eye flower and fruit.

'Golds' was a historic name for Corn Marigold.

Anagallis arvensis (Scarlet Pimpernel)

This is actually a native plant, and as such is adjusted to our climate, so can give great pleasure by being seen in flower right through a mild winter. It is almost prostrate, but could well be sown round the edge of a plot of taller flowers, or just accepted as an occasional weed in your garden. The little flowers open in sunlight. A variant *A. arvensis* ssp. *foemina* (Blue Pimpernel) is much rarer, but well worth trying to find, having blue flowers, sometimes with a red centre.

Anthemis arvensis (Corn Chamomile); A. cotula (Stinking Chamomile)

These are two of the native weeds which will add the 'white daisy' element to an annual mix without the complication of trying to use the invasive perennial Oxeye Daisy. Corn Chamomile is uncommon now, but Stinking Chamomile is still fairly widespread on heavy soils. Both have aromatic leaves.

Briza maxima (Greater Quaking Grass); B. minor (Lesser Quaking Grass)

These Mediterranean annual grasses are a wonderful addition to the garden if you are not upset by abun-

Weasel's-snout is an appealing weed.

dant self-seeding. They are most attractive, popular fresh or dried in flower arrangements, self-seed in soil, gravel, crevices, and look good among garden plants and in a wildflower mix. Their young leaves, usually up before Christmas, are bright green and soft to touch – they quickly become familiar so unwanted plants can easily be whipped out.

Chrysanthemum segetum, syn* Glebionis segetum (Corn Marigold)

Formerly a very common weed of the more acid soils in Britain and Ireland, this can still occasionally be seen turning whole fields golden.

Consolida ajacis (Larkspur)

This common garden annual was formerly an introduced cornfield weed in East Anglia, and the simple blue forms look well and mix appropriately with other arable weeds.

Echium vulgare (Viper's Bugloss)

County flower of East Lothian

A biennial, so plantlets could be brought on from seed and added to a summer-flowering mix. The tall blue spires with red colour in the buds and withering flowers are very attractive. Viper's Bugloss grows well in sandy and gritty soils.

Linum bienne (Pale Flax); *L. usitatissimum* (Flax)

The tall agricultural Flax has become familiar again as a field crop. In spite of the wonderful sky-blue flower colour, it is not a good garden plant because the flowers close after midday. However, it and its smaller native relative, Pale Flax, are worth adding to a mix because of their morning beauty (and agreeable round seed pods). Pale Flax can be perennial, but is best treated as an annual or biennial.

Misopates orontium (Weasel's-snout)

This is quite a modest plant, but its pink flowers show clearly that it is closely related to the *Antirrhinum* genus, and it has great charm. It grows best on neutral to acid soils.

Papaver argemone (Prickly Poppy); *P. dubium* (Long-headed Poppy); *P. hybridum* (Rough Poppy); *P. rhoeas* (Common Poppy)

County flower of Essex, Norfolk: Common Poppy

These are all red 'corn poppies', once an iconic part of the agricultural landscape, and still universally known. Prickly Poppy and Rough Poppy are both quite rare now, occasionally found in calcareous cereal fields ('prickly' and 'rough' refer to stiff hairs on their seed pods). It is worth adding any of them to an annual mix, though it might prove difficult to get seed of the rarer two. Organizations such as Plantlife, or your local Wildlife Trust, may have information about where to get it, and about local farmers who are helping with the conservation of our declining weeds. *P. somniferum* (Opium Poppy) is a splendid plant, but can rather overwhelm a wildflower mix, and is best treated as a garden plant.

Rare Corn Poppies: (left) *P. argemone* (Prickly Poppy) is small with narrow orange-toned petals; (right) *P. hybridum* (Rough Poppy) has rounder, pink-toned petals.

Silene conica
**in sand dune
habitat.**

A garden form of Opium Poppy.

Silene conica (Sand Catchfly)

This enchanting little plant has nothing to do with cornfield weeds, and is really quite a specialist, found only rarely on open, very sandy soils in the south of Britain. It is included here for gardeners who may have very sandy soil, or as a container plant which can be given a really sandy mix. It is a dainty, single-stemmed plant, rarely taller than 25cm, often much smaller, so although it self-seeds it is no problem to nearby plants.

Tanacetum parthenium (Feverfew)

In spite of much attention from herbalists during the last few decades, this has not turned out to be a particularly safe or successful migraine treatment, though as with many aromatics just sniffing crushed leaves, or inhaling from an infusion, can distinctly improve 'that headachy feeling'. Here it is recom-

Double and semi-double forms of Feverfew are pretty.

mended for its prettiness, and for its ability to pop up in really poor corners. The usual foliage is a bright, clear green with an umbel of pure white, gold-centred flowers. Some delightful variants are quite easily available; various doubles and 'Aureum' with golden leaves are among the nicest. Most gold-leaved plants will scorch in full sun, but otherwise Feverfew can be used anywhere, and will probably seed itself in places you have never thought of, but as it is very easy to recognize (the smell is so distinctive) it can be pulled out if necessary.

Almost irresistible? Field Pennycress.

Wild Pansy flowers have unpredictable colouring.

Thlaspi arvense (Field Pennycress)

This really is a weed, in both arable fields and gardens! As a young plant it is undistinguished, looking like Shepherd's Purse or other similar 'cressy' white-flowered annuals, but when its upright flowering stems develop their seed pods, it's a delight. Each fruit has a round green wing 1cm across, and in the sun some light shows through the wings. Plants would be nonsense in the border, but around the edges of a mixed annual patch, perhaps with Weasel's-snout, they would make a charming addition.

Viola arvensis (Field Pansy); V. tricolor (Wild Pansy, Heartsease); V. × wittrockiana (Garden Pansy)

These are all called 'pansies' but they are all tiny compared to the monsters grown as bedding plants, and as wild flowers they are complicated to sort out. Most violets are very promiscuous, which has been a joy for

gardeners because it has been easy to breed new colours and patterns, but when you see a little face among weeds it can be very difficult to know just what you have found. Wild Pansy has some respectable variants such as subsp. *curtisii* (Dune Pansy) with little yellow or pale blue flowers, found in west Britain and Ireland, and Field Pansy has recognizable tiny creamy flowers and is usually an arable weed, but many little wild pansies turn up like the raggle taggle gypsies, and are too difficult to name. They are pure pleasure though at the edge of an annual mix, or coming up unexpectedly throughout the garden. It is possible to source good colour forms, including black, and they are charming and easy to tidy up after flowering.

Perennials

Achillea ptarmica (Sneezewort)

This close relative of the familiar garden *Achillea* selections, which come from *A. millefolium* (Yarrow), has fewer and larger flowers, nearly always white. In garden conditions it runs, making it impossible to keep a good neat clump, but it does have two useful tolerances because it will grow in wet and acid soils. Double selections such as 'The Pearl' AGM are very pretty, and make wonderful cut flowers, otherwise Sneeze-wort is best in damp grass. It has also been used in developing hybrids with *A. sibirica*, such as the attractive pale pink 'Stephanie Cohen'.

Aegopodium podagraria (Ground Elder)

This suggestion always brings screams of horror, because ever since its introduction (probably in medieval times) as a green vegetable and gout medicine Ground Elder has been known as one of the most invasive of all garden weeds. However, 'Variegatum' which has cream and green leaves is extremely attractive, and looks beautiful in a low, wide container (which can have a plastic sheet or something underneath to stop roots burrowing down). This variety can also be let loose on a rough bank or among shrubs, though here it has the disadvantage of not being evergreen. It is quite widely available from specialist nurseries, one of which lists a really challenging variety named 'Dangerous'!

Angelica sylvestris (Wild Angelica)

Wild plants of this substantial 'umbel' often have attractive red or purple staining in the stems and flower parts, and the garden selections 'Purpurea' and 'Vicar's Mead' are well worth adding to a pond margin, stream edge or wet grass patch. As with most colour selections from wild plants, it is best to buy from a nursery you know, or at a plant sale so that you can see what you are getting. Seed-raised plants can be very variable, and may have reverted to the plain green ancestor – the 'Ravenswing' selection of *Anthriscus sylvestris* (Cow Parsley) is notorious for doing this. Candied angelica comes from the magnificent *A. archangelica*, which only occurs in Britain as a garden escape.

Centaurea nigra (Common Knapweed), *C. scabiosa* (Greater Knapweed)

The thistle-like purple heads of these plants are familiar from unimproved meadows, cliff grassland, road and track sides. They are too untidy for use as border plants in spite of their long flowering season, but are great on rough sunny banks, and essential if you do want to create some kind of flowery meadow. They are usually available as plug plants from firms which promote landscape restoration (this is much the most reliable way to introduce them, and saves several years). White forms of both exist, listed by specialist nurseries, with the large shaggy heads of the Greater Knapweed particularly attractive.

Chamaemelum nobile (Chamomile)

This must be one of the best known wild flowers – chamomile tea, chamomile lawns, chamomile seats... It occurs in literature, in herbal medicine, in garden books, and everybody loves it. Ironically, it is declining as a wild plant, now seldom seen except in parts of the West Country and the west of Ireland, and on ancient grazed land such as in the New Forest. It is a creeping perennial growing in damp short-grass communities, and used to be a typical plant of commons and of village greens where there was a pond and cottagers grazed their animals, but it has suffered a catastrophic loss of habitat during the past seventy years. It is actually a tricky customer in the garden, because it easily suffers from drought, and because its naturally creeping habit makes it difficult to organize as an edging. Dead flower heads quickly become unsightly, and garden varieties such as 'Treneague' which is selected to stay green, without flowers, can become quite sprawling when what was planned was a dense, velvety seat. To keep Chamomile growing low and thick, with its bright white flowers close to the ground, you really need a tame goose or sheep to graze your lawn, or be prepared to clip your seat with nail scissors!

This is not a low-maintenance species except when established in a damp lawn that is regularly mown – but because of the scent of its flowers and leaves (picked, walked on or just wafting on damp air) it is always desirable.

Claytonia sibirica (Pink Purslane)

This pretty little introduction began to appear in quantity in damp places in the West Country about seventy years ago. It is now widespread on road verges and lane sides, by streams and farm tracks.

ABOVE: **A rare sight now – Chamomile abundant on grazed common land.** INSET: **Chamomile flowers.**
BELOW: **Pink Purslane prettily self-established among garden ferns.**

Although it can produce dense patches, the rather squashy little leaves die down after midsummer, so it does not choke other plants, and it can be a delight in wet corners.

Crithmum maritimum (Rock Samphire)

Not related in any way to the annual *Salicornia* genus (Marsh Samphire) which is now popular in fashionable restaurants, this is a curious-looking umbellifer of seaside rocks and cliffs. Collecting it from the chalk cliffs at Dover is the dangerous occupation so vividly described by Shakespeare in *King Lear*:

> How fearful
> And dizzy 'tis to cast one's eyes so low!
> The crows and choughs that wing the
>   midway air
> Show scarce so gross as beetles; half-way down
> Hangs one that gathers samphire, dreadful
>   trade!

Now it is rarely eaten, having rather a rank taste with a hint of petrol, but in Tudor times it was pickled in vinegar and used as a relish to disguise the taints of unrefrigerated meat. It can still be used as a substitute for capers, to sharpen up bland or oily dishes. The leaves are fleshy and the flowers an interesting colour with tones of green, brown and yellow. It makes quite a striking rockery plant and is of course best in seaside gardens. Like many cliff plants, it likes to get its roots well stowed away in crevices or among stones.

Ferns

This group includes outstandingly beautiful plants that can define and decorate both natural land-forms and almost all styles of garden. Exotic species are popular, but there is tremendous scope for working with British and Irish natives. Ferns have a fascinating habit of 'throwing sports' – producing plants in strange shapes, some beautiful, some outrageous and grotesque, all remarkable. These can be propagated to remain true to the new form, and in the nineteenth century there was a famous 'fern craze'. British and Irish botanists scoured the countryside looking for these unusual forms, collecting and naming them, and many are still available. Fern collecting can easily become an obsession, but thanks to past enthusiasts there is a wide choice of native fern varieties available which make interesting and reliable garden plants. A useful point about native ferns is that some of the most desirable species are 'dry' ferns. There is a general belief that ferns are 'wet' plants, and can only be grown by ponds or rills and in special shade beds, and some do prefer humid conditions. Others, though, grow on hedge banks and cliffs, on scree, in disused quarries, on walls and even on grassy sand dunes. Semi-shade or even full sun may be tolerated, and though plants may droop in very dry weather (think of an Exmoor or Lake District lane-side in a drought) they come to life again as soon as it rains. Recommended species include:

Black Spleenwort – a small evergreen wall fern.

Athyrium filix-femina AGM (Lady-fern)

This extremely pretty deciduous fern does need damp ground, though some sun is acceptable. The plain species has delicate bright green spring leaves and is good for a bog garden, and lovely varieties with red stems are available. There are also plenty of different forms, including the quaint 'Frizelliae' AGM, found in Co. Wicklow in 1857, and sometimes called the Tatting Fern because the odd little pinnae (leaf lobes) are attached to the stem like lace.

Asplenium adiantum-nigrum (Black Spleenwort); *A ruta-muraria* (Wall-rue); *A. trichomanes* (Maidenhair Spleenwort)

These are some of the small ferns which decorate the crevices in old walls. They are delightful in walls, rockeries and the sides of steps, but like other crevice plants they need care to get them established because the roots have to be well inside the stonework where they cannot dry out too much. Because of this they are not widely available, but some specialist nurseries list them, and it is always worth looking when an old wall comes down.

LEFT: **Hart's-tongue has poise and is reliably evergreen.**
BELOW: **Native Shield-ferns and Male-ferns show lovely scales as they unfold.**

Asplenium scolopendrium, syn. *Phylittis scolopendrium* (Hart's-tongue)

A much larger fern than its tiny relatives and one of the most important for the gardener, this has many uses. It is reliably evergreen, essential in the winter garden and looks wonderful with Snowdrops or later with primroses or Wood Anemones. It will tolerate sun or shade, grow in woodsy conditions or on old walls and rockeries. There are some charming and readily available forms (known affectionately as 'scollies' to enthusiasts) including several of the 'Crispum' group which have decorative leaf tops, and the 'Undulatum' group with wavy-edged fronds.

Dryopteris affinis AGM (Scaly Male-fern); *D. dilatata* AGM (Broad Buckler-fern); *D. filix-mas* AGM (Male-fern)

This is a large genus, but these three classic tall ferns are all widespread, and are easily grown in the garden. Male-ferns can be grown in shade or in some sun and do not need especially moist conditions. They have tall, relatively narrow fronds and in time form

Young Royal-fern fronds look well in silhouette.

from early May when the tall stems make fine silhouettes before the fronds unfold, to October when the fronds turn a beautiful clear yellow before browning off. It is readily available, with several good forms, though the frequently offered 'Purpurascens' needs to be seen before purchase. It is variable, and sometimes the promised purple flush is barely visible, and just makes the plant dull-coloured.

Polypodium cambricum (Southern Polypody); *P. interjectum* (Intermediate Polypody); *P. vulgare* (Polypody)

It has to be admitted that ferns have less-than-romantic names, and these three are difficult to tell apart unless you are a good botanist. They are all included though because they prefer rather different soils, which helps in choosing one for your conditions. Southern Polypody likes lime, and grows in rocky limestone and old mortar. Intermediate Polypody is the commonest and is a very familiar sight covering West Country banks, and produces lusher growth than the other two. Polypody prefers woodland conditions, and can sometimes grow as an 'epiphyte' on mossy tree branches. The latter two species tolerate neutral to acid soils, and of course like leaf mould, and they all need free drainage. They are evergreen, and specially valuable in winter as the new fronds appear in the autumn. There are many selections: crisped, curled, lacerated, forked... this is a group that is easy to fall for.

Polystichum setiferum AGM (Soft Shield-fern)

Being evergreen except in very cold areas, this is the most important of the classic tall ferns. It will grow in full or part shade, although fronds may scorch in full sun, and it will tolerate most garden soils with free drainage (soggy conditions will rot the heart of the plant). This fern was also extremely popular with the Victorian fern hunters, and there are many forms though some are rarely available. One of the most beautiful of all, *P. setiferum* 'Pulcherrimum Bevis' AGM is luckily one of the easiest to source. Its slightly curving pointed fronds look wonderful with more stiffly upright ferns.

splendid clumps. Broad Buckler-fern has a broadly triangular frond, and does like at least moisture-retentive soil. All are deciduous, and have a fascinating range of weird and wonderful selected forms.

Osmunda regalis (Royal-fern)

This is the only fern on this list which really loves water. It grows beside, or even in boggy ditches, and in wet open woodland and willow carr. As its name suggests, this is a grand, tall fern, sometimes up to 1m, and is extremely decorative in a bog garden or by a stream or pond. It is deciduous, but looks good

Meadowsweet (like the surrounding Rosebay Willowherb) is a tough customer, possibly best left wild.

Filipendula ulmaria (Meadowsweet), *F. vulgaris* (Dropwort)

These rather dissimilar relatives are both lovely wild flowers, but have some problems in the garden. The familiar Meadowsweet grows in wet places, and is very vigorous, producing lots of leaf and having a relatively brief season in flower, so it can become a thug. The scent of the flowers is almost sickly, and the name actually comes from its ancient use to flavour a honey-based drink ('mead' not 'meadow'). An attractive pink form is available, but Meadowsweet is always a plant to treat with caution.

Dropwort is something of a different problem, growing poorly rather than too well in gardens. As a wild flower, on a chalk down or rocky limestone slope, it looks exquisite. The leaves with ruffled edges appear at ground level, and the thin-stemmed spikes of white flowers with delicious cherry-red buds stand about 35cm tall. However, it is another plant that flourishes in short well-grazed grassland, and in sunny, exposed places, where it needs to stay compact to survive. In the garden, if you can get it established with sufficient lime in the soil, it may lose this definition and become lax and droopy. The leaves

Dropwort has lovely rosy buds.

Dropwort is always more delicate than Meadowsweet.

may get mud-splashed, and the flower buds lose their glow. It is worth trying as a rockery plant, but can be disappointing in the border.

Fragaria vesca (Wild Strawberry)

Pretty and delicious, this miniature strawberry will flourish in almost any sunny place – on a bank, between flagstones, on the edge of shrubberies – but the native species does run and run. It's best in some unimportant spot where it can do what it wants, and is nice to grow up a bank or on a low earth-topped wall, so that you notice the berries before the birds do. A cultivated selection known as the Alpine Strawberry (*F. vesca* subsp. *vesca* f. *semperflorens*), which flowers and fruits right through the summer, is quite widely available, and is less likely to run, so makes a pleasant edging in a vegetable plot. However, its leaves are larger and coarser, and can lack charm. It is worth searching specialist seed lists for the 'white' berried forms (actually pale yellow), because birds do not 'see' this colour. *F. moschata*, the delicious Haut-bois Strawberry, is also occasionally available – all these little plants grow fast and easily from seed.

Frankenia laevis (Sea-heath)

This is not a heath, although its little leaves can be seen as look-alikes. It is actually in a genus on its own, and more closely related to a tamarisk bush than to a heather. It grows in dense prostrate mats on sand and saline muds, occasionally on the coasts of southern Britain. The little pinkish flowers are a dim colour, but the plant is included here for gardeners coping with problems of coastal exposure. It makes an excellent wall top or rockery plant in really bleak gardens, forming dangling mats of leaves, and can be used in sunny places as ground cover.

Galium odoratum (Woodruff)

This is an adorable little plant with evergreen ruffs of shiny leaves topped by pure white flower heads. It will tolerate shade, and dried stems and leaves produce coumarin, giving them the scent of new-mown hay. It was used as a strewing herb in smellier times, and a bunch can still make a room much more pleasant than artificial air fresheners can (though it is not long lasting). A dried leafy stalk soaked in apple juice gives a delicious flavour. However, Woodruff comes with a warning: it is an extremely invasive perennial, covering the ground quite densely and producing mats and tangles of wiry roots that are very difficult to remove. Growing it needs to be a careful decision.

Knautia arvensis (Field Scabious); Scabiosa columbaria (Small Scabious)

These are closely related to the familiar large-headed plants of gardens (which are mostly connected to *S. atropurpurea* or *S. caucasica*), but have much smaller heads that are nearly always a soft pale blue. Field Scabious can be tall, up to 1m at least in garden soil, and although it flowers throughout the summer it can end up looking very untidy, and the leaves are prone to white mildew in dry weather. It is really only good in tall grass. Small Scabious is a daintier plant, which can sometimes be seen in exposed places such as cliff grassland flowering on really dwarf plants. Its rosette leaves are quite attractive and the flower stems wiry and not inclined to flop. It should flourish in any

RIGHT: **A cause for admiration – Sea-heath flourishes in exposed places.**
BELOW: **Characteristic flowers of Field Scabious.**

sunny garden if there is some lime content in the soil. Various colour forms are available, including the pretty, cream-flowered *S. columbaria* subsp. *ochroleuca*.

Linaria repens (Pale Toadflax); *L. vulgaris* (Common Toadflax)

This is an endearing genus, their flowers with pursed lips like tiny snapdragons, and dainty tail-like spurs, but they are invasive. The yellow spikes of Common Toadflax are a familiar sight on roadsides, often forming large patches and flowering again after every mowing right up to the first frost. Pale Toadflax is less obvious, a smaller plant and less common, its flowers marked with beautiful dark veins. It grows on dry banks and in gritty waste ground such as railway sidings. Both are good in a really wild garden, but they will both creep and seed. You may already have the ubiquitous garden escape *L. purpurea* (Purple Toadflax), which is a gorgeous but uncontrollable plant that may have put itself in your garden whether you wanted it or not. If you decide to opt for life with the toadflax clan, they can be entertaining because they are extremely promiscuous, and can produce new colour shades with every generation.

The cheerful 'eggs and bacon' colours of *Lotus corniculatus* among seaside flowers.

Fragrant and inspiring – Hoary Stock in the Isle of Wight.

Lotus corniculatus (Common Bird's-foot-trefoil, Eggs-and-bacon)

This tiny creeping perennial is extremely common in short grass, and has heads of bright golden pea flowers opening from red buds. It is not substantial enough to grow on its own, but is bright and cheering in a flowery lawn.

Matthiola incana (Hoary Stock)

Another wonderful plant that may or may not be native, but is certainly a treasure. It also hovers between spring and summer, as in warm gardens it may start flowering in May though it has a long season. The flowers, white or rich purple, are clearly related to the single annual stocks of gardens (famil-

iar from childhood seed packets), but this species is usually a short-lived perennial, flowering for a couple of summers, and the plant itself is substantial. Young plants develop a bunch of leaves on an almost woody stem, stout like a cabbage, and from the leaves branches appear loaded with extremely highly scented flowers that last and last, and are perfect for posies. After flowering, long seed pods develop, which can be left on the plant till autumn and then the seeds can be saved. Young plants have pleasant greyish leaves. You can keep a population going by encouraging seedlings around the parent, or by potting on spares (which can be pinched out to encourage branching). The wild habitat is usually sea cliffs in southern England, where it is a rare but spectacular

Towering Cotton Thistles.

Surprisingly, Round-headed Rampion is related to Bellflowers.

Onopordum acanthium (Cotton Thistle)

This magnificent plant has been appearing in marginal habitats in England for hundreds of years, though it always appears too grand and stately to be a real wild flower, and is also a common garden escape. Its great silver stems can reach nearly 3m at times. Sometimes absurdly called 'Scotch Thistle', it is actually better known in the south of England and East Anglia. It is a biennial and seeds profusely.

Phyteuma orbiculare (Round-headed Rampion); *P. spicatum* (Spiked Rampion)

County flower of Sussex: Round-headed Rampion

Both of these plants are less common than most chosen for this book, and Round-headed Rampion is a bit of a specialist limited to open chalk grassland in southeast England. It has round, violet-blue heads, and like Sheep's-bit is related to bellflowers. Spiked Rampion is even rarer, once grown as a medicinal herb and now only hanging on in a few sites in the Sussex Weald. Both species are most attractive. Spiked Rampion has tall, pale yellow flower spikes

find, so sun, sharp drainage and exposure are good, but it will grow in most sunny borders. Plants don't stand upright – because of their cliff habitat the 'trunks' lean forward to avoid being blown down. You can stake them, but they look great flowering low down in the front of a border.

Onobrychis viciifolia (Sainfoin)

This very elegant member of the pea family has slender upright stems with pointed triangular heads of tightly-packed pale pink flowers. Leaves grow in a flattish rosette, and a group of plants is lovely in a border (they flower at about 35cm). A plant of open calcareous grassland, scattered across England as far north as Yorkshire, it can also be introduced to flowery lawns or 'meadow' plots, but it needs plenty of light and air and will not succeed among coarse grasses.

Quaintly shaped
Yellow-rattle
flowers.

and looks beautiful and mysterious growing in the damp semi-shade which it prefers (it requires acid soil).

Rhinanthus minor (Yellow-rattle)

This odd and charming plant is a 'hemiparasite', taking some of its food from the grass roots where it is growing. If you are interested in creating a grass plot full of wild flowers, this one can be established from seed after some preparation. The existing grass community needs to be repeatedly cut and raked, so that it becomes less dense. If there is rich topsoil where you are, some of this needs to go too – this is a good principle for all 'meadow' gardening, because it will discourage coarse grasses from becoming dominant again and overcoming the flowers. When the ground is almost bare, sow some Yellow-rattle, and keep mowing, raking and topping up with seed for a couple of years. It is hard work getting it going, but once a patch is established the Yellow rattle will keep the grasses in order by pirating some of their nutrients. It seeds abundantly, the dry heads making the 'rattling' sound, so you can keep spreading it. Seed may sometimes be available from landscape restoration nurseries, or you may know a place where it is abundant and the farmer generous.

Very small but very sweet – Heath Pearlwort in flower.

Sagina subulata var. *glabrata* (Heath Pearlwort)

This is a less than spectacular wild flower, and you may feel that it is much too close to its relative *S. procumbens* (the pesky Procumbent Pearlwort which makes irritating little mossy mats all over paths and flower beds, and is difficult to weed out). However, Heath Pearlwort is a more sedentary species, and in flower has lots of charming little white flowers on its flat leaf mat. A garden selection *S. subulata* var. *glabrata* 'Aurea' is widely available, has golden foliage, and is pretty in paving stone crevices or at the edge of steps.

Sanguisorba minor, syn. *Poterium sanguisorba* (Salad Burnet); *S. officinalis* (Great Burnet)

Both of these plants can look lovely in natural settings, but may disappoint in the garden by growing too lush and flopping about. Salad Burnet had a great vogue in the 1970s and '80s as a pot herb, and indeed there is no harm in any part of the plant, but most people took the name too literally and munched down the rather tough and uninteresting leaves in salads. It was actually popular throughout history for flavouring drinks, and can be used to give the cucumber flavour to Pimms. Gerard (1597) said that it would 'make the heart merry and glad ... being put into wine' and adds the nice thought that 'it yeeldeth a certain grace to the drinking'. We might now reach for the Sauvignon Blanc without bothering about the burnet, but the idea is pleasing. Great Burnet has had a more recent fashion, being one of the plants associated with the 'prairie' style, and many other *Sanguisorba* species and selections are available to gardeners. Some of the cultivated varieties have the dense heads of darkest red which distinguish our native, but if you want to grow it, remember that it hates being too dry. A selection, 'Pink Tanna', is reasonably compact.

Scilla autumnalis (Autumn Squill)

We do not have many native bulbs, so some gardeners like to grow both this and Spring Squill. This one is small and inconspicuous, found mostly on the coasts of southwest England, and flowers without leaves. At close quarters it is delightful, with flowers in shades of mauve and soft violet, but from head height it is quite hard to see. It is best grown on an exposed rockery, at eye level, or in an alpine pan to be viewed at close quarters.

Autumn Squill has refined colouring.

Neat and stylish – Saw-wort flowers.

Serrratula tinctoria (Saw-wort)

Christopher Lloyd (2000) called *S. seoanei* (the species most often seen in gardens) 'A charming plant, which people notice in spite of its modesty', and the same applies to our native Saw-wort. The small purple flowers are thistle-shaped, but the plant is not prickly, and each part is neat and compact. It prefers neutral to acid soils, and does not need to be too dry.

Sibthorpia europaea (Cornish Moneywort)

This is a plant strictly for West Country or Co. Kerry gardeners who cannot resist local oddities. It is an uncommon plant which grows in damp rocky or grassy places where it is partly shaded and never suffers drought. Cornish stone-built banks and the stone walls edging field tracks in Ireland make good habitat, and it is also found on stream sides. As a garden plant it has become a lawn denizen, and can sometimes be found established in moist corners. At Trebah Gardens, near Falmouth, it may be spotted growing most enchantingly as an epiphyte on some of the old tree fern trunks in the valley as well as in mown grass. The minute purple flowers are barely visible, and the tiny round leaves grow at ground level.

Spotting the tiny flowers of Cornish Moneywort is a challenge (a playing card would hide this whole patch).

Silybum marianum (Milk Thistle)

Like the Cotton Thistle, this magnificent Mediterranean alien has been around for centuries, and can look quite wild in marginal habitats such as quarry edges and hedge banks. It is usually biennial, which is an advantage in the garden because the most decorative aspect is the leaves, which have extremely spiny borders round beautiful shining green leaves boldly marked with white. Even a young plant is decorative, particularly in early spring. Flowers are the usual purple thistle 'shaving-brush' shape (a white form, 'Adriana', is occasionally available) but the bracts of the flower head are sensational, with dramatic spines, so that a bud is shaped like some terrifying medieval weapon. Limy, well-drained soil is good, and full sun is required.

All parts of the Milk Thistle are dramatic.
ABOVE: **magnificent white-streaked leaves;**
INSET: **impressive bud cases.**
BELOW: **The button heads of Devil's-bit Scabious look good in large groups.**

Succisa pratensis (Devil's-bit Scabious)

With *Knautia arvensis* (Field Scabious) and *Scabiosa columbaria* (Small Scabious) this completes our trio of closely related natives with rather similar, usually blue, flowers. The name 'Devil's-bit' seems to come from the root, which looks as if the end has been bitten off, but stories vary about why the Devil did this. It also has a number of local names involving buttons, which is more explicable because that is exactly what the neat round flower shape suggests. Colour variations are reasonably common, so pink and white can be found as well as the usual purplish blue. Wide-

ABOVE: **Salsify flowers open in the morning.**
RIGHT: **Goat's-beard.**

spread in unimproved grassland throughout Britain and Ireland, this plant will tolerate most soils if not too dry. The little button heads get lost in a border though, and show best close-planted in grassy plots so that the colour can be seen at a distance.

Tanacetum vulgare (Tansy)

Although impossible to separate from images of old-fashioned gardens, this is actually a native plant that was frequently brought in and out of gardens for use both in folk medicine and to repel various creatures including parasitic worms, mice and bluebottles. The crushed leaves do have a clean, astringent smell. There are a number of garden selections with gold or variegated leaves, but some of these seem to fade away, some to revert, and some to behave thuggishly,

so it is probably safest to treat them all in the same way as the basic form – plant where it can decorate some rough grassy bank and can spread if it wishes. It does not spread at great speed, but is a tough customer to remove if you do have to. Grigson (1958) mentions its centuries of popularity, but says, 'it is still worth growing for the golden buttons, the fern-like leaves, and their warm, refreshing, spicy aroma'. Books of country recipes sometimes include rhubarb tansy, a dish that can be nicely flavoured with this herb, if used cautiously.

Thymus polytrichus (Wild Thyme); T. pulegioides (Large Thyme)

There are so many garden varieties of creeping thymes available that there is little need to go to great effort to obtain the native species, as most of the selections will give a similar effect. Wild Thyme creeps in very short grass, on bare chalky banks and over exposed rocks, and the most popular garden use is planted between paving stones or on rockeries, where it will make low spreading mats. Forms are available with pink or white flowers and darker or paler purples, and a number have variegated or gold foliage.

Tragopogon porrifolius (Salsify)

Once grown as a vegetable, this entertaining plant can occur on waste ground, and is established in marginal habitats such as the sea walls of the Thames Marshes. It has dramatic purple daisy flowers, which open for the morning only, and interesting smooth grassy leaves reminiscent of a large *Allium*. It will seed around, and is most enjoyable in grass that is not cut till July, because it will give interest after bulbs have died down; it also stands well above Oxeye Daisies, so

in spite of the short ration of colour-hours, some gardeners welcome it. Our native species, *T. pratensis* (called 'Goat's-beard' after its dandelion-like seeds), is much smaller with rather dingy yellow flowers. It has nice old local names like 'Jack-go-to-bed-at-noon', and is quite quaint if examined closely, but is too inconspicuous for garden use.

Valeriana officinalis (Common Valerian); *V. pyrenaica* (Pyrenean Valerian)

Our Common Valerian has attractive cut leaves and tall stalks topped by bunched pale pink flowers. It prefers damp soils, and can look wonderful grown in a stand near a pond or stream, or on a grassy bank. Its Pyrenean cousin is a finer plant, found only as a rather rare naturalization in England and Scotland. Up to 2m tall, it is good in a damp shrubbery or wild garden.

AUTUMN AND WINTER

From the beginning of October until the New Year very few new flowers appear, although many native plants will keep going until there is a really sharp frost. These need not be dull months for the gardener though, as many of our native shrubs have attractive berries and leaf colours and autumn can be their most valuable season. Winter gardening too need not be a matter of scrabbling for interest, but can be planned for stylish effects — several native ferns are evergreen, and look fine with bare shrubs, and plants such as Butcher's-broom are at their most interesting around Christmas, while the spiny or whippy silhouettes of Gorse and Broom keep a furnished look for banks and shrubbery edges. Mixed hedges using native plants may not look spectacular at other times of year, unless you have abundant Dog Roses or Honeysuckle, but autumn can reveal a real tapestry of colours. Getting this effect is not difficult, and the research can be most pleasantly done by walking lanes, fields or commons as near to home as possible, finding hedges with a variety of shrubs and seeing what the most characteristic local bushes are. The oldest hedges will generally have the widest variety, and this in itself is interesting, because each different species is thought to represent about a hundred years in the life of the hedge. Very old boundaries may still incorporate many of the species originally growing when fields were first cleared, and hedges beside old roads will have had centuries to accumulate still more from the pips, seeds and scraps left by travellers and their animals.

Native woody plants have had a start on perennial

OPPOSITE PAGE:
Autumn – Traveller's-joy and Guelder-rose berries.
RIGHT: **Butcher's-broom berries in snow.**

Autumn gold –
Field Maple.

wild flowers in coming into trade – local councils and road authorities have had public pressure to use them for some time – so many tree nurseries and landscape firms will stock a selection, and can probably give advice on suitable plants for your area, if trudging lanes is not practical for you. As well as their use in hedging, some of our native shrubs will grow to specimen size, as small trees; others, such as Spindle and Guelder-rose, are quite handsome enough for mixed shrubberies.

Acer campestre (Field Maple)

ACERACEAE *(Maple family)*

This modest shrub or small tree is our only native maple, and gets very little attention in the gardening press. Decorative Japanese maples, and the spectacular North American species are much better known, while the ubiquitous *Acer pseudoplatanus* (Sycamore) is actually only a neophyte, a giant weed introduced in the sixteenth century and now all too common throughout Britain and Ireland. However, Field Maple is well worth considering for use in a garden hedge,

or if you have space enough for a wild garden, as a specimen tree. It is a widespread native in England and Wales, north to about Co. Durham, on clays and calcareous soils. Elsewhere it will originally have been planted. The flowers are yellowish green and blend with the dainty new leaves, so the early summer appearance is pretty (and it is unlikely to grow large enough to tower over your car, dropping sticky nectar), while the autumn colour is superb, the leaves turning very pure tones of red-gold or yellow. Winter twigs have slightly corky bark. Several garden selections with variegated leaves are available (though it is hard to beat the basic species for autumn colour), and some nurseries have delightful variants with red keys or stems.

Berberis vulgaris (Barberry)

BERBERIDACEAE *(Barberry family)*

This is a scattered and elusive shrub, probably originally a garden escape (it has been recorded as a relic of medieval gardens), but like so many *Berberis* species it is certainly garden-worthy. It has drooping racemes of yellow flowers, followed by red berries which are said to make an excellent jelly. William Robinson (1870) relates that 'The prettiest brake of shrubs I ever saw was an immense group of the common Barberry at Compton Winyates, laden with berries weeping down with glowing colour.' The inner bark is bright yellow, and in accordance with the Doctrine of Signatures it was used to treat jaundice, the yellow disease, but Barberry remained popular for its candied berries and delicious preserves long after this chancy way of prescribing medicines was abandoned. Like many *Berberis*, mature growth is multistemmed and tangled, and the twigs are very thorny, so it is most easily managed as part of a hedge.

Bryonia dioica (White Bryony)

CUCURBITACEAE *(White Bryony family)*

This odd plant twines and scrambles like a jungle liana, but the stems die down in the winter. These habits are similar to those of our other 'Bryony', *Tamus communis* (Black Bryony) and the names may trace back through many changes to a Greek word *bruein* meaning 'to grow luxuriantly', which well describes how both plants may ramble through and over hedges. Botanically they are very different though, because White Bryony is related to cucumbers, and Black Bryony to lilies! At close quarters the bristly maple-shaped leaves and scrambling vines of White Bryony, as well as the pale greenish flowers, are reminiscent of aspects of this family of vegetables. It is included here because it has very fine red autumn berries. The nurseryman Walter Ingwersen (1951), who had a great eye for inventive ways to use plants, points out that it is our only British member of the gourd family, and like them, 'It is a rapid climber and I have seen it used for covering arbours in continental gardens... The root grows into an immense many-legged parsnip sort of thing, for which reason country people regard it mistakenly as the Mandrake.' Indeed it was historically used as a cheap substitute for expensive imported Mandrake, *Mandragora offic-*

inarum, in various potions for encouraging conception, and Grigson (1958) relates a fascinating detail about a former advertising practice using White Bryony: 'The root was child-shaped, or could be trimmed to look like a child; and Bryony mandrakes in human form, sometimes sown with grass seed to give them hair, used to be suspended in the English herb-shops...'. Its speedy growth and good autumn berries are, however, its only real garden uses, and Ingwersen is probably right when he says, 'unless you wish to use it as a seasonal covering of something better hidden, I should advise you not to bother with it'! Setting scattered plants in a native hedge is probably the most practical modern use.

Traveller's-joy has the typical seed heads of *Clematis*.

Clematis vitalba (Traveller's-joy)

RANUNCULACEAE *(Buttercup family)*

Also known as Old Man's Beard (and many other local names to do with beards and whiskers) our only native *Clematis* cannot really be recommended for the garden because it is extremely rampant. Quite frequent in southern England, scattered elsewhere, it is always obvious where it occurs because it is so vigorous, and can cover hedges, trees, banks and buildings with great curtains and swags of twiggy vine, showing up in autumn when the leaves die back and the feathery seed heads catch the light. Sometimes places like disused quarries can disappear beneath almost unbroken carpets of Traveller's-joy, though the name comes from earlier times when land was more used and managed, and its presence in roadside hedges would have been more familiar than on abandoned ground. It is worth observing though, because it does sometimes look lovely, and a number of small-flowered and species *Clematis*, such as *C. flammula* from southern Europe, can be grown in similar 'wild' styles to good effect on trees and in hedges.

Colchicum autumnale (Meadow Saffron)

LILIACEAE *(Lily family)*, subfamily 3 – WURMBAEOIDEAE

This is a wonderful plant – thrilling in the wild, decorative in the garden, with odd and mysterious habits and a fascinating history. Its most commonly used English names, Meadow Saffron and Autumn Crocus, are both pretty useless, because it yields no saffron (which is made from the anthers of *Crocus sativus* in Turkey), and in spite of its appearance is not even related to crocuses, which are members of the Iridaceae (iris family). Much more to the point are some of the old local names, such as 'Naked Ladies', because they emphasize the startlingly nude appearance of the pearly pink flowers and white 'stems' as they appear leafless from the ground. The 'stem' is actually the tube of the flower, which holds the reproductive parts dealing with giving or accepting pollen, while the ovary lives safely underground in the corm until carried up by the spring-growing leaves to form a pod. It's a clever, secretive strategy, but it is sometimes possible to get a look at some of the workings by examining the bulb racks in garden centres in the autumn. Spring bulbs come into stock when many *Colchicum* species would be flowering, in September, and flowers may start to develop on the shelf. Seeing

The lovely 'naked' flowers of *Colchicum autumnale* **may be abundant.**

the corm in its shiny brown tunic, with the buds beginning to elongate, it's easy to see that they are single organisms – elongated flowers rather than flowers and stems. Corms like this will grow perfectly well if planted, even if this first flowering produces some mis-shapes.

Found mostly in central and southern England, and very rarely in southeast Ireland (where it may be a medical archaeophyte), this was formerly a very abundant plant, growing in huge populations in damp meadows, sometimes in rides and glades in managed woodland (which sometimes leaves relict plants hanging on in shade). It was also frequently grown in gardens, not for its beauty alone but because all parts of the plant contain powerful toxins including colchicine, which was, and still is, used in medicines to relieve gout. It has suffered a huge decline in the past century, partly because of these same toxins that make the leaves poisonous to grazing stock, so farmers have eradicated it whenever possible. The leaves are also considered ugly by some gardeners. Robert Gathorne-Hardy (1961) notes: 'it has the drawback of large, broad leaves which come up untidily in spring', but he says its flowers are essential, so suggests that 'a few bulbs at least must

Spring value – handsome *Colchicum* **leaves around a pruned apple tree.**

go into the border, perhaps in the places reserved for annuals, which will come up with the leaves, and later hide their decay'. It can be worth treating them boldly, making a spring statement with the leaves – they can look handsome and effective.

There are many cultivars and foreign species, some very rare, available from bulb lists, and *C. autumnale* is quite widely available. There are white and double forms, and 'Nancy Lindsay' AGM is an excellent strong colour. The white form is sometimes known as 'Dog's Bones' (spoken more often with affection than scorn) because the bare flowers coming up do look just like little white bones left in the shrubbery. Corms can be planted in managed grass or as rockery or border bulbs, and are good among shrubs as long as they are not in very deep shade.

Cornus sanguinea (Dogwood)

CORNACEAE *(Dogwood family)*

The Dogwood genus is very familiar to gardeners because many hybrids and cultivars are extremely spectacular, such as the variegated form of *Cornus controversa* with its horizontal branching, making it look like a wedding cake; or the many varieties of the North American species *C. florida* where the flowers are surrounded by showy pink or white petal-like bracts. Our native species is much more modest, but still both attractive and useful. It is common as a hedge plant and in scrub on calcareous soils (including heavy clays) throughout most of central and southern Britain, more local in southern Ireland, and an introduction elsewhere. The twigs are dark reddish-crimson, and like in some willows, first-year growth is the brightest. This gives great interest in a

Rich autumn colour in the native Dogwood.

clipped winter hedge, and in sunny places the colour often appears in the leaves as well, deepening to a rich dusky purple in autumn. The berries are black and inconspicuous, but in a regularly clipped hedge there is often a second flowering in autumn, the small umbels of creamy flowers showing up over the dark leaves. The wild plant of *C. sanguinea* is stiffly upright with crimson twigs, but it is worth investigating some of the cultivars because some are much daintier and more low-growing, so very suitable for small gardens. There is a group of Dutch selections, sold with rather interchangeable names ('Midwinter Fire', 'Winter Beauty', 'Winter Flame') which are quite spreading little bushes with twigs in delicious colours of orange-yellow, apricot and coral. Bressingham designed a classic winter container of one of these dogwoods underplanted with Snowdrops and 'Black Grass' (*Ophiopogon*), and the pretty twig colours do go beautifully with a number of early small bulbs. These have the added advantage of being quite slow-growing, and keeping their twig colour as they expand, so they do not need (in fact they dislike) annual cutting back.

Three other dogwoods are sometimes naturalized in Britain. *C. alba* (White Dogwood) and *C. sericea*

(Red-osier Dogwood) are familiar as park and road-side plantings, and their suckering habits sometimes cause them to spread and naturalize. *C. alba* has many named selections, and is the most important species to use for winter colour, because the bark can vary from black ('Kesselringii') to many shades of red, and there are attractive gold and cream leaf variegations. Among the best are *C. alba* 'Aurea' AGM with leaves in gentle gold tones; *C. alba* 'Sibirica' AGM (formerly 'Westonbirt') with brilliant red bark; *C. alba* 'Spaethii' AGM with red bark and creamy variegated leaves, which is good in all seasons. All these need management, and a third of the twigs should be cut out each year to keep fresh, bright growth. *Cornus mas* (Cornelian Cherry) is occasionally seen established in hedges. It seldom produces its cherry-like berries in Britain, but its ochre yellow flowers on bare twigs in early spring are delightful, and it is well worth trying in a hedge or as a small tree.

Lamb's-tails – Hazel catkins are a favourite sign of spring.

Corylus avellana (Hazel)

BETULACEAE *(Birch family)*

Nothing could be more familiar, even if you live in a town, than the idea of catkins and hazel nuts, but this shrub is not necessarily considered suitable for mod-

Corkscrew Hazel adds fascination to the winter garden.

ern gardens. Hazel has a very, very long history with humans, because it is useful in several ways, and it must have been one of the earliest of woodland plants to have been managed. Because young branches are both strong and pliable, it was perfect for making hurdles and fences, and for making the framework of 'wattle and daub' walls. Even better, it can be managed as a rapidly renewable crop – a hazel stool cut down will sprout masses of shoots (just as willows do), and these can be cut at whatever length or thickness you wish. This use, growing coppice wood, has continued throughout history and is still done, for hurdles and pea sticks and garden art in particular. Coppice cycles, when a grove might be cut down at certain intervals, also provided an essential habitat for woodland flowers because it guaranteed a 'top up' of daylight every few years. Add to this the excellent food value of the nuts, and the hazel is clearly seen as one of our most essential native plants. Management for coppicing, or growing substantial

trees to harvest the nuts, can only be practical for landowners or people lucky enough to have really large gardens, but there are some variants which will fit in quite small spaces.

In about 1863 a Lord Ducie found a strange bush in a lane near his home in Gloucestershire. It seemed to be a Hazel, but twigs and branches were twisted in bizarre shapes. He was interested enough to have it moved into his garden, and this is what we now know as *Corylus avellana* 'Contorta', the Corkscrew Hazel, sometimes called 'Harry Lauder's Walking Stick' after a Scottish singer popular on early radio. This shrub is very slow-growing, and can even be kept in a large container for years. One of the most irresistible moments for seeing Hazel catkins is against the blue of a winter sky on a rare fine day, and the Corkscrew variant provides this treat with the extra fascination of the twisted twigs in silhouette.

There are also variants with red or purplish leaves, such as 'Fuscorubra' or 'Red Majestic', which make

Glastonbury Thorn braving winter weather.

Crataegus laevigata (Midland Hawthorn); *C. monogyna* (Hawthorn)

ROSACEAE *(Rose family)*

Our native hawthorns are very alike, from a gardener's point of view, and are really most relevant as hedge plants. Hawthorn in blossom appears at the end of the Spring chapter, because the saying 'Cast not a clout 'ere May be out' is still used to define the moment when spring turns to summer. Grown in a tightly clipped hedge there are the advantages of very effective thorny protection, bright fresh green leaves, and some blossom and berry interest, though to see a good display bushes have to have some top growth. Autumn leaves may go a rich red, and of course the crimson berries (the 'haws') are both decorative and a valuable winter bird food, especially for migrant thrushes such as redwing and fieldfare. Midland Hawthorn, which will grow in light woodland as well as in the open, has some selections with pink or red flowers, such as the double 'Rosea Flore Pleno' AGM and 'Paul's Scarlet' AGM. These are pretty and familiar from street or park plantings, and widely available, but the most fascinating variant for gardens is *C. monogyna* 'Biflora', the Glastonbury Thorn (or Holy Thorn).

Double whammy: Hawthorn leaves and berries may colour up.

good shrubbery plants if you can get them settled with enough light, but not so much exposure that the coloured leaves scorch. 'Pendula' has weeping branches, while 'Heterophylla' has rather peculiar cut leaves (and is a bit of an acquired taste). There are also a number of selections grown for their nuts, though many of these such as the famous 'Kentish Cob' come from the continental species *C. maxima*. Hazels enjoy lime, and will grow happily pushing their roots through stony soil.

Richard Mabey in *Flora Britannica* (1996) summarizes the wealth of stories and superstitions surrounding this remarkable bush, but the most important fact for gardeners is that it flowers, and fruits, twice a year. Traditionally this happens at the ordinary time in late spring, and again just before Christmas, when sprigs are cut from one of the Glastonbury Abbey trees to send to the Queen. However, some of the grafted bushes (available from nurseries) may flower more than twice, and at almost any time of year. Whenever it happens the effect is really interesting, as leaf, flower and fruit are all present at once, even if winter weather sometimes gives them a slightly battered look. The Glastonbury trees in the Abbey grounds have been propagated by cuttings since the seventeenth century, and have grown there throughout the centuries, except for one hiatus when the Puritans destroyed the main bush because of its idolatrous and Papist associations. It had frequently been snipped by religious pilgrims though, so the line was restored from one of these souvenirs. There are also trees on nearby Wearyall Hill, and the Glastonbury Thorn proved its iconic position in public consciousness when one of these was vandalized in the winter of 2010, and this cruel act reached the national news. 'Biflora' is available from specialist shrub nurseries (the RHS *Plant Finder* always lists stockists), and can be grown as a specimen tree or kept trimmed to a smaller size.

Euonymus europaeus (Spindle)

CELASTRACEAE *(Spindle family)*

The native Spindle is widespread in Britain up to central Scotland and in the north of Ireland, introduced elsewhere. *E. japonicus* (Evergreen Spindle) and *E. latifolius* (Large-leaved Spindle) are also familiar shrubs because they have been used in hedges and gardens for many years and often persist from old plantings. *E. europaeus* prefers calcareous or base-rich soils, and does best in fairly light situations as a hedge plant or

Daring colours – berries of native Spindle.

at a woodland or shrubbery edge. For most of the year it is inconspicuous – it is deciduous, with brown bark, developing quite plain mid-green leaves and tiny green flowers – but it does produce the most spectacularly beautiful berries of any native shrub. The brilliant orange fruits are held in a bright pink case, rounded and ribbed like a miniature pumpkin, which is pretty enough itself when it turns coloured in autumn, but looks really amazing when it splits to show the contrasting fruit colour.

Fruits and capsules often hang on into the winter, looking very decorative, and there are a number of cultivars which provide a range of berry colour and varying good autumn leaves. Among them *E. europaeus* f. *albus* has white capsules; the leaves of the yellow and white variegated 'Aucubifolius' get delicious pink tones in autumn; the classic selection 'Red Cascade' AGM fruits generously on attractive arching branches and becomes a real beacon of red leaves and berries. Spindles can be incorporated in mixed hedges or grown as specimen shrubs or small trees.

Occasionally plants will become spectacular in another way, because there is a fairly widespread British moth, the Spindle ermine moth (with the

Wonder or horror? Ivy covers an old copper-mine building in the Quantocks.

rather astonishing scientific name of *Yponomeuta cagnagella*) whose caterpillars may cover whole sections of hedge or substantial bushes with tents of densely spun silk, inside which they live while eating all the leaves. The infested plants look pretty miserable that autumn, but the stripping is unlikely to do lasting damage. *Butterfly Conservation* are reassuring in their website text and literature, describing an infestation as a 'very occasional minor and temporary nuisance... control should not be necessary... the affected shrubs usually recover'. Spindle is quite a frequent hedge plant in parts of Somerset, and the silk 'tents' may be seen here and there every few summers, but the bushes are perfectly healthy the next year. The moth itself is a small, pretty white creature with a scatter of black spots on its silky-haired wings. Some of its ermine moth relatives can have more serious effects on crop trees, such as apples, but the

Spindle ermine's erratic appearances need not put gardeners off growing Spindle. Visitors to a garden, or local hedge, will probably be really excited and interested by the sight of the silk-wrapped twigs, and the only likely cost is one autumn's leaves.

Hedera helix (Ivy)

ARALIACEAE *(Ivy family)*

Nowadays, Ivy is one of the most reviled of our native plants. It is considered to be the home-owner's enemy and undesirable in gardens. A sight like this ruined building in Somerset (above) is considered a blot on the landscape by many. Like Giant Hogweed and the various plants labelled (usually incorrectly) 'Deadly Nightshade', and like most toadstools, Ivy is believed to be 'out to get us', and these beliefs make a sad statement about the increasing separation between us and our native flora. A look at some of our most enlightened botanical and garden writers shows that Ivy has long caused people to take sides, and has raised quite passionate controversies, but that the writers themselves are usually devoted fans. It has also been important in art and literature for more than 2,000 years, acquiring symbolic meanings as well as being appreciated for its leaf shapes and way of growing, and in these associations it has usually been valued rather than reviled. Mabey (1996) includes fascinating material about the myths that have gathered around Ivy (just as the plant can surround a tree), and he very sensibly starts by looking at some of the modern versions, and how they influence popular beliefs.

One of the most persistent 'bad plant' theories is that Ivy is a parasite, sucking nutrients out of supporting trees. This is completely untrue: it feeds itself by roots and photosynthesis like any other plant, and its little suckers are purely for climbing and stability. Trees covered with Ivy only die if they were going to anyway, and the worst effect of a big growth of the creeper is mechanical – a great weight and spread of evergreen leaves at the very top of a weak tree may be enough to fell it. As Bowles (1915) noted, 'The worst of old ivy-covered trees is that some day the tree gets too rotten to hold the weight and over the whole thing goes.' Alternatively, some picturesque 'ivy-tods' with their billowing growth of evergreen leaves may be a dead tree actually held up by the Ivy, and this can apply to walls as well. Much of what Ivy does, or can do, is interpreted in the eye of the beholder. As Mabey points out, that can be influenced by your profession, or even where you live. 'In the gale-dashed West Country and the territories of commercial foresters it is regarded as a curse and a killer of trees. In less turbulent eastern regions and amongst more easy-going gardeners and naturalists it is looked on benignly, as an ornament to buildings and woods and a boon to birds and bees.' This is a very fair summary, and it is well worth examining some of the positive aspects.

William Robinson (1870) had no reservations: '... the best of evergreen climbers is our native Ivy [which]... for edgings, banks, forming screens, cover-

Unplanned decoration – variegated Ivy explores a garden shed.

ing old trees, and forming summer-houses should be made far larger use of'. He also recommends 'Ivy-clad wigwams... and covered ways', and points out that we are lucky to be able to grow this useful treasure, because countries further north are too cold. Robert Gathorne-Hardy in *The Native Garden* (1961) devotes a whole chapter to Ivy, giving the plant what can only be described as a 'rave review', partly for what it has contributed to his own memories and love of art, but also praising its many uses in the garden: '... the familiar five-pointed leaves grow only on the clinging or creeping stems. When it climbs into full daylight the Ivy puts out simpler foliage, and on these upper stems, in late autumn, flowers open to satiate the last hunger of the bees. If these simple-leaved stems are struck as cuttings, the resulting plant will put out only those leaves, and will usually lose its climbing habits;

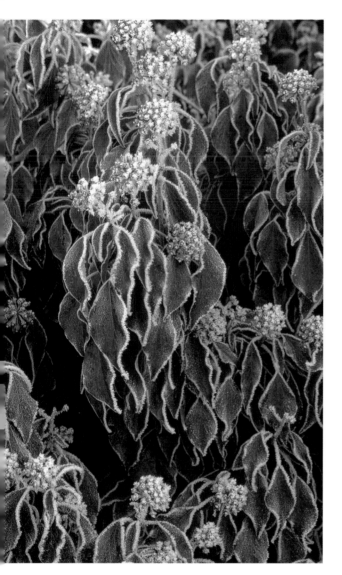

Art and nature – Ivy outlined in hoar frost.

it to the ground, allowing the delicate display to compose itself all over again.' Christopher Lloyd was enthusiastic too. In *Foliage Plants* (1973) he wrote: 'Ivies can be used in a great many different ways: on walls, of course, and on trees, which they won't really damage at all... Ivies are good ground cover, both in sun and in shade and they can also be used to scramble round the base and lower branches of deciduous shrubs, providing winter interest where there would otherwise be none. There need never be a fear of them getting above themselves... because you can choose your varieties for vigour according to how much work you want to do.'

It is clear from all these authors that they share an attitude that is ruled by common sense: Ivies are wonderful plants for carrying out both bold and subtly graceful ideas, and if things go wrong you can just cut them back or pull them off. Jane Fearnley-Whittingstall (1992) in her beautifully produced monograph, begins the very first paragraph: 'Ivy is a plant of almost miraculous versatility and adaptability', and it is encouraging to hear reports from twenty-first-century garden visitors of striking uses of Ivy in modern gardens. For instance in the fascinating Shropshire garden which is the subject of *The Morville Hours* (Swift, 2008) visitors have admired perfect carpets of ground-growing Ivy, even and unbroken, looking startlingly effective under tall shrubs or trees, while another Shropshire garden, reknowned for its Snowdrops, features a glorious bush of the yellow-berried 'Poet's Ivy' (*H. helix* f. *poetarum*), grown over a tree stump and in full fruit while the *Galanthus* are in flower, so echoing the tones of the rare 'yellow' group. There are a number of *Hedera* species available, but many of the most fascinating and appealing plants are variants of the native *H. helix*. Some of the favourites are shown in *Shrubs* (Phillips and Rix, 1989) and their page of leaf samples shows clearly how wide the choice can be, with size, shape and colour important, in countless combinations. Most garden writers have their personal favourites, and many descriptions are available; there are also several National Collections (information available through *Plant Heritage*). There is only one warning about buying Ivies – many of the pretty varieties seen in garden

in this way may be contrived rounded bushes of dark-green leaves....' These 'Ivy Trees' are quaint and appealing in a wild garden or shrubbery, and it is also useful to know of this trait if you are considering Ivy sculptures. This author also loved seeing young growth on a plain background such as a smooth-barked tree, where 'the stem climbs in graceful irregularities, and the uncrowded leaves are wonderfully set off by the quality and colours of the trunk', and he used to leave the Ivy until 'becoming too thick, it obscures its own pattern. Then, if I remember, I strip

Pollen-rich flowers are followed by plum-black fruits.

centres are likely to be intended for indoor growth, and are probably bred from tender species.

One aspect of Ivy which is rather losing ground in the national consciousness is its use in winter festivals. It used to be considered as essential as Holly for Christmas decorations, but this importance seems to have slipped during the last century. Grigson (1958) commented on this: 'We have forgotten the Ivy which once had a magical power. So Ivy is no longer the *sine qua non* of Christmas decoration, and the inevitable companion of the Holly.' There are suggestions from folklore that Ivy may have lost popularity because it has been a historic victim of sexism! Traditionally the showy Holly with scarlet berries signified masculinity while the modest Ivy was more feminine, and this may be why in the well-known carol *The Holly and the Ivy* we sing 'Of all the trees that are in the wood / The Holly bears the crown...'. Grigson also adds wryly that Ivy being out of fashion is 'A pity, because you do not have to purchase Ivy at an outrageous cost from

the greengrocer, and you can fix it easily round the house, where the umbels, with or without berries, make delicious starry patterns against the walls'. Perhaps it would be a worthy sustainability project to re-launch Ivy trails for green Christmases, and revive the romantic and poetic associations whose banishment from modern life is lamented by the same author: 'Ruins, owls and Ivy go together – or they did until the Ministry of Works decided that ruins were all to be historical exhibits; picked, pickled, pointed, and sterilized.'

However, Ivy does now have important groups of supporters nationally because of its flowers. Bee-keepers and naturalists are really being heard in opposition to the guardians of tidy bricks and mortar because of the many current threats to pollinating flying insects. E.A. Bowles (1915), a meticulous observer of his garden near Enfield, was well aware of this aspect of Ivy nearly a century ago, when he described a September stroll in *My Garden in Autumn and*

Winter: 'We must stop a moment... to admire the carpet of fallen Ivy blossom that covers the gravel under the large bush of golden-leaved Ivy just under the windows of the morning room. Many wasps and drone flies... are sucking away at the ovaries of many flowers... and their constant movement causes a shower of petals to fall as we watch.' He recalls 'the pleasure of visiting [this bush] after dark with a... lamp to see if I can pick up a rare moth or two among its numerous nocturnal visitors'. The late flowering of Ivy, sometimes into November, makes it a hugely valuable source of nectar and pollen for countless insects preparing for hibernation, and for bees in particular, now that so many problems and dangers affect them.

Humulus lupulus (Hop)

CANNABACEAE *(Hop family)*

Hops, beer, the slanting funnels of oast houses in a landscape in Kent or Herefordshire... some of the most iconic images in the consciousness of what identifies 'England' come from this plant, and its associations twine into art and a national sense of place just as its vines can twine into a hedge when it is growing wild. It is a native plant but it is also widely naturalized after centuries of being grown as a crop. However, there is some hidden history connected with Hops, and its accepted 'Englishness' is the product of a certain amount of spin. From prehistoric times people made alcoholic drinks with whatever was available to them, and there is plenty of archaeological evidence for beer- and wine- making from grains and wild fruits from the time of the first farmers in Britain. However, on this very long time scale, the use of Hops to flavour beer (which is still based on fermented grain) is positively modern, and was in fact discovered by the Dutch. Hops were being cultivated in Holland from the ninth century (during years when the two countries were quite often enemies), but were only really introduced to English brewing in early Tudor times, and were not at all popular at first

with conservative beer experts. However, their use makes it possible to keep beer for much longer than if it is made without, so they became an essential ingredient as trade increased and goods could be moved more easily. Now English Hop gardens are quite a rare sight, and the trade is only supported by loyalists in the Real Ale movement, because they can be grown far more cheaply in Eastern Europe.

Hops make a beautiful garden plant though, and can be grown in most garden soils, though they are vigorous climbers and need space. Both commercial and decorative varieties exist, including the ever-popular gold-leaved 'Aurea' AGM. They can be grown through hedges, up trees and bushes, on walls and fences, and of course the heads are wonderful for flower arranging, whether fresh or dried.

Hypericum androsaemum (Tutsan)

CLUSIACEAE syns. GUTTIFERAE, HYPERICACEAE – *(St John's-wort family)*

This subshrub with yellow flowers and shining berries (red ripening to black) is characteristic of dampish woods and shady hedge banks in southwest England in particular. It is not particularly striking, seldom taller than half a metre, and only keeping a few winter leaves when growing in sheltered habitat, but the autumn berries are attractive and good for flower arranging, and it is a tough plant, well able to put up with dreary corners (as long as they are not too dry). It has a long history of use in herbal medicine, and was considered beneficial for many conditions, though some of its popularity came from a mistaken identification (it was confused with a famous Mediterranean medical plant *Vitex agnus-castus*). Its most common English name, Tutsan, may have come from Norman French *toute-saine* meaning 'all-whole-some'. There are several garden selections that have good berries and attractive leaf colours for both summer and autumn. These include 'Albury Purple' and f. *variegatum* 'Mrs Gladis Brabazon'.

Holly is great for gardens – a gold-variegated cultivar.

Ilex aquifolium (Holly)

AQUIFOLIACEAE *(Holly family)*

'The Holly and the Ivy' must be two of the best-known plants in Britain and Ireland, and there is no doubt that in modern popular consciousness 'The Holly wears the crown'. With Mistletoe it has become the most essential bit of Christmas stuff, its berries matching the colour of Father Christmas's suit, Rudolph the Reindeer's nose, a Robin's breast – all the festival reds of millions of cards and decorations. This reputation is not just a Victorian invention like many of our Christmas images, but comes originally from very ancient beliefs. Grigson (1958) wrote 'both Holly and Ivy were plants with power, and they were specially suitable for protection in the dead of the year…'. The colour red was believed to be a defence against evil, and the red berries of *Sorbus aucuparia* (Rowan) and *Crataegus monogyna* (Hawthorn), as well as of Holly, were used to ward off witches and ill-fortune by planting trees close to houses and cow byres. Holly's reputation was almost universally as a benign plant,

and its beauty was acknowledged. Even Henry VIII wrote a song with the refrain:

> Grene growith the holy, so doth the ive;
> Thow winter blastys blow never so hye,
> Grene growith the holy.

The name is ancient, from the Old English *holen* or *holegn*, and can still be found in place names such as Holne, Hollingworth or Holmwood (though this cannot always be told at a glance, because of similar Old English words for 'hollow' and 'hole'). In Cornish the name was *kelen*, and Grigson quotes the example of Pencalenick, 'head of the Holly place'.

In gardens, *Ilex aquifolium*, the common native species of Britain and Ireland, gives us a huge choice of wonderful shrubs. There are Hollies with no prickles, Hollies with hedgehog extravaganzas of spines, Hollies with a multitude of different variegations in gold, cream or white, tall Hollies, short Hollies, and so on. They can be grown in mixed hedges, clipped as topiary, crown-raised as specimen trees, or used as colour highlights in shrubberies. They are endlessly rewarding, and it is possible to find at least one for every kind of garden. There is one key fact though which must be known before you make your choice: hollies, our own species included, are dioecious, having male and female flowers on different plants. Females have the berries, so if these are what you most want, you need to make sure that the plant you choose is a female, and that there is a male tree somewhere nearby so that the bees can do the pollinating. The male flowers are creamy-white, in clusters tight among the leaves; they come out in spring and have a pleasant scent. Named cultivars are always one or the other, and reliable lists such as that found in the RHS *Plant Finder* will have (f) for female and (m) for male after the names, and so should the labels in garden centres, but the names themselves are sometimes irritatingly misleading. For instance 'Golden Queen' AGM is a male plant, while 'Silver Milkboy' is female. There are several National Collections (details from Plant Heritage) and that at the RHS garden at Rosemoor in north Devon, where the hollies are incorporated into the display plantings, is accessible all year round. The former Curator of this garden and collection, Chris Bailes, has written *Hollies for Gardeners* (2006) which is a 'must' for anyone interested.

Iris foetidissima
(Stinking Iris, Gladdon)

IRIDACEAE *(Iris family)*

With *Iris pseudacorus* (Yellow Flag) this is one of our only two native irises, and it is rather a different character from its tall, water-loving relative. It is also less widespread, being something of a western speciality, most familiar from woods and hedge banks in southwest England and Wales, and usually found on calcareous or base-rich soils. Although botanical books usually translate the Latin name literally, as 'Stinking Iris', the name in most common use is 'Gladdon', which may have come in roundabout ways from Old English *glaedene*, which itself comes from a diminutive form of the Latin word *gladius*, a sword. So

Gladdons are named for their sword-shaped leaves.

this Iris shares a descriptive name meaning 'little sword' (from the shape of the leaves) with the genus *Gladiolus*. The other name still in occasional use is 'Roast Beef Plant', which ties in with the 'stinking' label, because if you crush the leaves the smell released does suggest meat, though it is more like the raw smells in an old-fashioned butcher's shop than anything roasted. Writers and gardeners who grow the plant agree that the whole 'stinking' idea is unfair, because unless the plant is attacked – leaves crushed or torn – there is no smell at all. Grigson (1958) calls it 'A maligned species... its curious smell of raw beef... it keeps to itself, or in itself, until you crush the dagger-like flags'. A more justifiable complaint from some gardeners is that it seeds so widely. Birds do not eat the seeds, but in hungry months blackbirds in particular may have a go, scattering them around, and they do come up in plenty. Luckily they pull up easily, so an overabundance can be avoided with little effort.

The flowers are admired by some, ignored by others, and they admittedly come in quite sombre colours, matching the ambience of the shade they often grow in. Robert Gathorne-Hardy (1961) calls them 'an inconspicuous purplish colour', though he does also say they are 'shapely and beautiful'. Walter Ingwersen (1951) mentions 'a rather sad violet blue' as the commonest form. Grigson is more poetic: 'The pencilled lead-blue or lead-purple of the flowers is snakish or dragonish', though he does also quote Gerard (1597) who described 'an overworne blewish colour, declining to greyish, or an ash colour'. Their most interesting feature is the fine dark veins on the falls, and their frequent variability is fascinating. There is a pale yellow form (usually quite expensive to buy) but it is really less atmospheric in a shade bed or woodland garden than the normal plant. For most gardeners, however, the flowers are quite unimportant, because it is the seed heads that matter. In late summer the flowering stems produce large green capsules, quite interesting in themselves, which gradually split and open wider to display the brilliant orange seeds with their fascinating hint of vermilion. These remain on the plant for the three months till Christmas, the capsules only gradually drying to straw colour. Ingwersen praises the 'brightly orange-coloured large seeds which are revealed by the bursting seed capsules... they are the great glory of this otherwise inconspicuous plant'. Gathorne-Hardy agrees: 'In autumn the Iris forgets its modesty; the pods, drying and drooping, open to reveal... large seeds of a bright orange-red.' Grigson compares them to 'small blood oranges, set in rows', while A.E. Bowles (1915) with his artist's eye, noted that this is one of the few plants which 'produce red seeds inside green pods', and this effect in early autumn is particularly striking.

Gladdons, in common with other irises, can get Iris Rust. This is a fungus called *Puccinia iridis*, which the RHS *Pests and Diseases book* (1997) says is 'encouraged by wet weather', and is common during West Country 'summers'. It is a bore, because the unblemished leaves are smart and shiny but begin to look shabby when stained by groups of tiny orange pustules. It is not dangerous though, and the only

Ripe Gladdon seeds in autumn sun.

Wild Gladdons with leaves marked by iris rust.

treatment needed is to cut off the most unsightly leaves – the plant is unhurt and will grow more. Wild plant diseases can nearly always be viewed in a relaxed way; their hosts have after all evolved through millennia to be good survivors, and this rust develops only after the seeds are formed and the important part of the year's work has been achieved. It disappears in winter, so this evergreen iris can take advantage of any winter light with new, undamaged leaves.

Gladdons can be grown in shade, even quite dry shade, but also in semi-shade or full sun (though the shining leaves look best when not scorched by exposure). Christopher Lloyd (2000) suggests tucking them away 'under a shady wall or hedge bottom' where they will provide acceptable dark green leaf colour, but not be too noticeable if they get rust-marked. The seeds really are spectacular, so the most important choice when planting gladdons is to ensure a clear view during the autumn months. They are wonderful in flower arrangements, and are usually still good to add to Christmas decorations.

Ligustrum vulgare (Wild Privet)

OLEACEAE (Ash family)

Wild Privet is really a very nondescript shrub. It is found through most of Britain and Ireland except in the north of Scotland, most often on base-rich soils, growing in hedges and scrub. It can be semi-evergreen, has small black berries, and its most distinctive character is the strong scent of the creamy flowers, particularly noticeable in the evening. Some people find this sickly, but for others it is intensely evocative of midsummer. It is easily trimmed, and makes an adequate addition to a mixed hedge (Mabey, 1996, quotes a record of it being planted as 'every fifth bush' in Enclosure hedges at Frampton on Severn in 1815), though the Japanese species *L. ovalifolium* (Garden Privet) is now much more commonly used. Garden and botanical writers have almost nothing to say about Wild Privet, so why is it included here?

Privet flowers smell too sweet for some people.

Because it provides an inoffensive way of taking an exciting gamble. Wild Privet is the principal food plant of Britain's largest resident moth, *Sphinx ligustri* – the Privet hawk moth – which has magnificent pink, black and brown wings, while the caterpillar is a startling lime green. The moth is not usually found north of the Humber, but if you live in southern England, you might be lucky enough to attract it, putting a rather dull bush to thrilling use!

Lonicera periclymenum (Honeysuckle)

CAPRIFOLIACEAE (Honeysuckle family)

County flower of Warwickshire

Honeysuckle needs no introduction. Its twining growth and pretty flower heads, each graceful curving flower tube with a drop of nectar in the base, are

Honeysuckle in a traditional flowery hedge.

an equally familiar sight in countryside hedges and town gardens, and the wonderful scent is always popular. We find Honeysuckle, in name at least, in hundreds of everyday objects and materials, in soap and scent, in wallpaper and fabric designs, air fresheners and hand creams. Honeysuckle has featured in art, literature and songs for centuries, and a garden arbour covered with roses and Honeysuckle is a cliché for a romantic setting. It presents no problems for the gardener, though foresters sometimes complain about it (as they do about Ivy) for 'choking' trees. In the garden our native species and its named selections can be used in many ways, as a managed hedge plant, as ground cover, as a really tall climber on a pole or tree-trunk, and to disguise fences and sheds. It will grow up from shaded roots to find its own sunlight, and can really be cut back at any time – plants in hedges clipped in late summer usually burst into flower again during the autumn. William Robinson included a section in *The Wild Garden* (1870) called 'The Fence Beautiful'. Praising what he called 'live

fences' (that is hedges) as 'beautiful as well as enduring and effective', he suggested 'tying together' the stiffer shrubs with 'graceful climbers', of which 'none surpass our Honeysuckle wreathed over a fence.' The idea can be practical even in town gardens, because a dense hedge with some prickly shrubs in it is indeed good security, but also because such a hedge can be grown to disguise the ubiquitous larch-lap, and eventually to replace it. Honeysuckle on its own, if it is growing strongly, will also weave itself a 'trunk'. Bowles (1914) describes a 'tree' in his garden which puzzles visitors with its 'narrow pillar of growth' and 'yellow trumpets hanging in mid air'. This was actually a Honeysuckle grown to hide completely the spindly trunk of a weak conifer, whose branches only appeared high above. This climber can also be grown on a wire frame, as a pillar or shaped sculpture, the trailing shoots knitting together over time to make a self-supporting structure. Gathorne-Hardy (1961) liked it as a ground cover, and it can sometimes be seen as such in woods, where it is pleasant in winter because in shelter it may keep some leaves – these can develop reddish 'frost colours'. This author liked to mix it with *Vinca minor* (Lesser Periwinkle), which is properly evergreen, near the edge of wood or shrubbery so that both plants could creep towards sunlight to encourage flowering.

Honeysuckle has rather sticky red berries, pretty enough but usually quickly grabbed by birds, and its garden advantages remain its scent, its prettiness in flower, its ability to repeat flower in autumn, and the ease with which its creepers can be managed to be both useful and attractive. Many species and hybrids of *Lonicera* are stocked by nurseries and garden centres, including plenty of named selections from *L. periclymenum*. Some have quite rich tones of red and pink in the buds and flowers, having been selected for having stronger colours than the wild plant. They include the widely available continental selections: 'Belgica' with purplish trumpets, which flowers early (sometimes in May) and again in late summer; and 'Serotina' AGM, sometimes called 'Late Red'. Two selections with paler, more subtle colours are 'Graham Thomas', found in a Warwickshire hedge in the 1960s, and 'Sweet Sue', found by Roy Lancaster and named after his wife. Both of these are almost white at first, the flowers yellowing when open, and each has good scent.

Malus sylvestris (Crab Apple)

ROSACEAE *(Rose family)*

The real native Crab Apple is only included here 'because it can be'! All apple blossom is sweet to see, and the little green fruits do have a pixy charm, but not only is it much less garden-worthy than the many cultivated hybrids available, but it is very hard to identify. Apples have been eaten by people since prehistoric times, and cultivated almost as long, so they have been selected, interbred, escaped from gardens, been left in abandoned orchards, had their cores chucked in the hedge by generations of travellers, and been eaten by trillions of birds. So the 'wild' apple, which may be found in a wood or a hedge, may have a very complicated gene pool, after many early crosses, often with *M. domestica* (syn. *M. pumila*) the ordinary apple, which is an ancient introduction, itself of hybrid origin. Descendants of these crosses look very like the Crab Apple. It takes a brave botanist to make a study of 'wild' apples, and around Britain and Ireland pure *M. sylvestris* is probably the least likely apple to be found. For native plant purists, some specialist nurseries do stock it, but if you just want blossom and pretty miniature apples to look at or make jelly from, there are plenty of choices if you consult a specialist nursery. Of course, there is also great interest now in historic varieties of *M. domestica*, and varieties connected with particular counties or even districts can be traced.

Prunus padus (Bird Cherry); *P. spinosa* (Blackthorn)

ROSACEAE *(Rose family)*

Plums and cherries have also been eaten by humans as well as by birds since prehistory, and grown since gardening began. Like apples, wild and domestic species have become inextricably mixed up, crossed, re-crossed and back-crossed through all the chances of life. Blackthorn, whose fruits are sloes, is native, but there is another group with miniature plum-like fruits that are widespread in hedgerows and scrub. These are *P. cerasifera* (Cherry Plum), *P. cerasus* (Dwarf Cherry), and *P. domestica* (Wild Plum), which incorporates among its subspecies *insititia*, the Bullace or Damson. All these have met and crossed many times, and can anyway be variable, so trying to sort them out can be highly technical. Regions which had plenty of Norman settlement, such as Co. Wexford in south-east Ireland, often have all kinds of 'wild plums' in old hedges, and this is clearly evidence of history rather than of plant geography. All of them, and of course Blackthorn, can be used in hedges, or allowed to

Wild Bird Cherry flowering in Scotland.

A fine form of Bird Cherry at East Lambrook, planted by Margery Fish.

grow into small trees. *P. cerasifera* is the first to flower, as early as February in the south, while *P. cerasus* flowers prettily with new leaf in April. *P. spinosa* is a familiar sight when the white flowers seem to lie on the leafless twigs and branches like snow, and this is the source of the term 'Blackthorn winter', when a surprise cold spell strikes in late March or April when spring *should* have arrived. Blackthorn is extremely spiny, with really sharp strong spikes, and makes a very protective hedge (handle with care when trimming!). The generic Irish word for Hawthorn, *Sceach*, was loosely used in southeast Ireland (not a Gaelic-speaking area) in the last century for any big thorn. Children were most afraid of a Blackthorn *sceach* because the tip of the spine might break off in a puncture wound, making it go septic. The fruits are of great value for sloe gin, and for making jellies, but Blackthorn has gathered something of a nonsense reputation (and a threat to its abundance), by becoming associated with the 'begorrah' element in Irish tourism. The knobbed sticks called 'shillelaghs', with which all joke Irishmen are supposed to bash heads, were originally made from various woods including Oak and Holly, and have historical records of being used in nineteenth-century London, but not in ancient Ireland! However, Blackthorn wood is strong and knotty, and it gained the reputation for being *the* proper wood for a fighting stick. Modern sticks are now to be found in many tourist shops, and the poor Blackthorn, which is quite a slow-growing shrub, is suffering from being irresponsibly harvested to make them. Like Hawthorn, Blackthorn flowers are believed to be unlucky if brought indoors.

Bird Cherry is a mostly Northern species, and in flower it is obviously garden-worthy, producing very abundant slightly drooping white racemes of almond-scented flowers. Spring leaves are a fresh green, so the effect in May is charming. It can be grown in a shrubbery, or kept to one stem to form a specimen small tree. The 'cherries' are black, and rather unpleasant tasting (though perfectly harmless) and as the name suggests birds enjoy them. There are some excellent named selections including 'Colorata' AGM which has gorgeous purple and copper tones in the young shoots and foliage and pinkish flowers, and 'Watereri' AGM, produced by the famous Knap Hill nursery in Surrey in about 1914, which has massive racemes.

Ribes alpinum
(Mountain Currant)

GROSSULARIACEAE (Gooseberry family)

This charming but little-known shrub has none of the characteristics that put people off some of this genus. Gooseberries have fierce thorns, Flowering Currant has scented flowers, which get compared to all kinds of nastiness, a number of the species have aromatic leaves, but this little bush is both scentless and thornless, having small racemes of yellowish-green flowers, red berries, and very neat leaves on upright branches. Growth is densely twiggy, so it makes an excellent hedge plant, and it is extremely shade-tolerant. It is quite uncommon as a wild bush, found only in rocky limestone habitat in north Wales and the north of England, but it is much more widely established as a garden escape, and there is no reason why it should not be grown elsewhere as long as your soil is not really damp and acid. A number of specialist nurseries list it. The berries are not spectacular, but if you want them try to grow several plants, because the male and female flowers are like Holly, on separate bushes. A named selection, 'Aurea', has golden new leaves, and can be grown near the front in shady shrubberies or at the back of a fern bed, because it is reasonably compact and usually becomes wider than it is high.

Dog Rose hips.

Rosa canina agg. (Dog Roses);
R. pimpinellifolia, syn.*
R. spinosissima agg.
(Burnet Roses)

ROSACEAE (Rose family)

County flower of Hampshire: Dog Rose

For a field botanist, reading 'agg.' after a plant name is something of a danger signal, because it is short for 'aggregate' and means that there can be many species and subspecies gathered under this one cover-name, and only an expert will be able to tell them apart. For various reasons several native plants are in this category, including Brambles and Dandelions, but it need cause no problems for a gardener. The famous line by American writer Gertrude Stein (1913), 'Rose is a rose is a rose is a rose, is a rose' is more to the point because roses are such a matter of personal taste, whether they are wild species or garden hybrids, historic or just launched at Chelsea. Our native roses can be simplified into essentially two main groups, which have quite different styles of plant, and this simplification makes a practical starting point for choosing what to grow in your garden.

'Dog Roses' are the familiar single roses seen in hedges or scrub, in shades of pink or near-white, and producing scarlet hips in autumn. They used to be

ABOVE: **One of the many species of wild rose,** *R. sherardii* **in Sutherland.**
RIGHT: **Simple and sturdy – 'Heavenly Rosalind' bred by David Austin to keep casual looks.**

quite central to life, particularly during the Second World War, because the hips contain high levels of Vitamin C. Country people had made rose-hip jelly for centuries, and during the years of rationing and poor food this was provided by the state (along with concentrated orange juice and cod-liver oil) to keep babies and toddlers healthy.

People knew where rose bushes were plentiful and valued them, though now they usually only get a passing glance when they come into flower, and farm and council hedge cutters account for many of the hips. There are many variations within the aggregate, and the north of England and Scotland in particular

Burnet Rose on the Burren.

It is often only about knee height, unless it has some shelter, and has creamy flowers, masses of soft prickles, and deliciously fat black hips. It is the most important ancestor of the 'Scotch' roses, and there are some historic selections that were found in the wild such as the 'Dunwich Rose' from Suffolk. Scotch roses often have masses of small flowers, sometimes semi-doubles with pink and white streaks, and make informal thickly twiggy bushes with very pretty small leaves. They turn up at local plant sales, often without names, because they can be propagated from their freely produced suckers, and there are some enchanting plants among them. There are also a number of hybrids under the name *R. × harisonii* which have slightly larger flowers and include 'Williams Double Yellow', and many of the available commercial bushes are larger and more loose-growing than the wild plant.

If you are thinking of using native shrubs in a wild garden or in mixed hedges, the roses are invaluable. They are disease-free, can be pruned at any time, have two seasons of interest with flowers and hips, and of course the thorns are good protection on town garden fences. The ins and outs of their identities may be daunting, but that makes no difference to their good nature and usefulness. After all, 'Rose is a rose...

have some lovely types with much pinker flowers than usual, and interesting hairy hips. In the south, the main variant to look out for is the 'Sweetbriar' type, which has wonderfully aromatic leaves, and can be found on specialist nursery lists as *R. rubiginosa*. There are several modern cultivars in the 'English Rose' group, which have been bred to have the simplicity (and disease resistance) of our native roses. Like the wild species they can be grown as shrub roses, on fences, or as part of a mixed hedge.

The other native rose which is important in gardens is the Burnet Rose. This is a much smaller shrub, found round the coasts of most of Britain and Ireland, growing in exposed habitat such as limestone pavement, cliffs, grassy sand dunes and limestone heath.

Ruscus aculeatus (Butcher's-broom)

LILIACEAE *(Lily family)*, subfamily 8 – ASPARAGOIDEAE

This dignified little stiff, evergreen subshrub is one of the oddest plants in our native flora. It is found in woods and shady places, scattered across Wales and southern Britain. It is never common, and probably its most secure stronghold is the New Forest where it grows in open woodland under Beech or Oak, or occasionally among bracken in more scrubby habitat. Incredibly, it is closely related to lilies, but even the one clear clue it may give to this, its berries, will only be recognized by gardeners lucky enough to have a

Butcher's-broom in the New Forest.

Fascinating details – flower, berry and cladode of Butcher's-broom.

mature asparagus bed. It is, however, an excellent garden plant, and worth close examination. First of all, the 'leaves' are not leaves, but the stems flattened out (with a sharp spine on the end). They do all the work that leaves usually do, are very tough and enduring, and are structures called 'cladodes'. The tiny flowers appear in mid-winter, opening from a minute chaffy knot in the middle of a cladode. They are reasonably easy to see on a mild, bright day, but the plant has a fascinating ability to turn its cladodes over in hard frost so that the flowers are sheltered underneath the blades.

Like Holly, Butcher's-broom is 'dioecious', having male and female flowers on different plants. There are a few selections in cultivation which have both kinds of flowers, and it is well worth searching them out;

otherwise several plants are necessary. The berries develop during the summer, shiny and green, but look at their best when coloured up in winter.

The English name Butcher's-broom does suggest that the stiff, spiny branches could have been used for scouring wooden butcher's blocks, but the idea lacks well-founded reports, and it is hard to imagine that masses of branches could ever have been so readily available. The berries may actually give more of a clue, because they are known to have been used to decorate festive meats. In the garden it is valued as a stylish front-of-shrubbery plant, looking good with or without berries. Robert Gathorne-Hardy (1961) had no male plant: 'I have two females living the life of nuns.... Nevertheless the bush is satisfyingly beautiful in form without the adjunct of berried glory.' He also valued its ease of propagation, pointing out how 'the stem is creeping and new specimens can be chopped and dug from the edge of an old one.' This really is a welcome quality, because although a clump will increase gradually, it never runs enough to be a pest.

Modern garden selections have naturally concentrated on berry production. A hermaphrodite form is listed quite often, and there is a very appealing dwarf called 'John Redmond', which berries freely and is a delight for small gardens and shady rockeries.

A spring icon – 'Pussy-willow' catkins.

Salix (Willows)

SALICACEAE *(Willow family)*

Willows are too big a subject for this book, and many of the species grow too big for ordinary gardens, but the catkins ('pussy-willows') are iconic in the spring countryside, and there are few more useful plants in the British and Irish floras. Willows, birches and Hazel were among the first and most abundant woody plants to recolonize these islands after the last ice age, and for hunter-gatherers and early settlers willows had many uses. The 'withies' can be used for weaving into baskets, for making frameworks for mud walls, into baskets, for making frameworks for mud walls,

Characteristic silhouettes of pollard willows.

for making fencing hurdles; strong but flexible young twigs can be used almost like rope to tie joints and bundles. Many uses continued throughout history – because willows sprout easily from a cut stool, producing twigs of working length in a short time, it is really the ultimate renewable resource. Pollard willows, mature trees whose crown branches are cut back regularly, used to be a familiar sight in many parts of Britain, growing along ditches and streams, and sometimes lasting for many years, hollowed out but still producing new growth. A comment from a Romney Marsh shepherd, made in the 1980s, gave a glimpse straight back into history when he described following his father along the dykes where they would tap the trees with their crooks 'to hear if the baby Wrynecks would hiss'. These shy birds liked to nest in the hollow trunks – now they and the pollards are all too rare.

Over the turn of the twenty-first century there has been a great revival in the use of willow, and in areas such as the Somerset Levels withy beds are again quite a common sight, producing rods for making into hurdles and fencing, for many forms of 'garden art' and for 'living willow' constructions, as well as for basket weaving. Thousands of holiday makers heading for the West Country must look forward to seeing the shapely figure of Serena de la Hey's giant Willow Man beside the M5 motorway at Bridgwater – the Somerset friend of the Angel of the North – and withy

Work and play – commercial withies stacked under an ornamental weeping willow in Somerset.

beds can be seen from the Paddington–Penzance train near Taunton. In Ireland there is also an ancient tradition of willow use (traces of prehistoric craft objects and artefacts are sometimes found preserved in bogs), and in this country as well as in parts of England 'Sallies' was the name most commonly used for willow bushes and trees ('Sally' = 'sallow' = plants from the genus *Salix* = '*saileach*', Irish for willow), and when W.B. Yeats famously wrote his poem 'Down by the Salley Gardens' ('Gort na Saileán'), published in 1889, he may have been thinking of withy beds. This poem, inspired by a fragment of old verse collected by the poet in Co. Sligo, has become a much-loved, still-popular song, words and melody attracting singers and composers (from Benjamin Britten to Órla Fallon) throughout the last century.

There are eighteen species of native willow scattered through Britain and Ireland, and because some of them interbreed very easily, this figure can be multiplied by at least three in any attempt to add up all the possible varieties. However, some of the most familiar, such as *Salix fragilis* (Crack Willow), a favourite for making cricket bats, can grow into huge trees unsuitable for gardens. Others, such as *S. viminalis* (Osier) are best as crop plants, not ornamentals, and look too coarse among garden shrubs. The two most common 'pussy' willows, which are also known as 'palms' in some parts, and are carried to celebrate Palm Sunday, before Easter, are *S. caprea* (Goat Willow) and *S. cinerea* (Grey Willow). They are both tough and aggressive colonizers, good in managed damp hedgerows but much too invasive and untidy for the garden. Some of our mountain willows,

Lighting up
the winter –
Salix alba
var. *vitellina*
'Britzensis' AGM
at Westonbirt.

which are much rarer, are very beautiful. The quite closely related *S. lapponum* (Downy Willow) and *S. lanata* (Woolly Willow) both have delicious silvery-haired leaves on dwarf bushes, but they are tundra plants, and not at all easy to grow in lowland gardens. *S. reticulata* (Net-leaved Willow) has green leaves with exquisite veining, and grows almost prostrate, but comes from a specialized habitat on damp mountain ledges quite unlike a normal rockery. So there are not many native species that are obvious recommendations for normal gardens. *S. purpurea* (Purple Willow) is probably one of the best, being reasonably dainty and having lovely purple tones in the bark of bare twigs. It can also be cut to size, but will rapidly sprout again. There is a weeping form available, 'Pendula' AGM, and 'Nancy Saunders' has good colour and pretty little catkins. *S. alba* (White Willow) can be managed as a small pollard for pond edge or shrubbery, and there are some attractive garden forms, kept looking good by regular cutting back. A form with wavy twigs, 'Dart's Snake', can look interesting in a winter garden, and selections with coloured bark can be used to spectacular effect.

Sambucus nigra (Elder)

CAPRIFOLIACEAE *(Honeysuckle family)*

Elderflower wine, elderberry wine, preserves flavoured with the 'green' fragrance of the blossom, the heavy scent on midsummer walks, the rank leaves crushed to keep flies away from people and horses, the pithy dry twigs hollowed to try to make whistles, a bush planted beside a house or cow byre to keep witches away – the Elder is another native plant that has been, and still is, closely connected with our lives.

Elder has recently become an unlikely high-fashion plant in gardens. Wild bushes occasionally produce variegated leaves, and forms such as the white-flecked 'Pulverulenta' have been in cultivation for centuries. There are many forms available now, with gold leaves, with white, cream or green-shaded variegations, with purple leaves and pinkish flowers, with yellow berries or green berries (though the latter are a touch inconspicuous!). An excellent selection is f. *laciniata* AGM which has handsome cut leaves – it can get rather large, but Elders can be cut down each

ABOVE: **Elderflower means summer.**
BELOW: **Simple but sophisticated – Cut-leaved Elder.**

year (like *Buddleja*) if necessary, and bushes are in any case not long-lived. As garden plants Elders are tolerant of most conditions. Semi-shade is best for varieties with pale leaf colours – all variegations are inclined to scorch, but need some light to bring out the colour –

GOOD AND BAD MAGIC

Elder has always had an ambiguous reputation. It used to be credited with various healing and protective properties, but had to be used carefully as it could attract the Devil as well as turn him away. Although the flowers are wonderful the wood is poor, bushes grow in weedy places, and bruised leaves stink. Its grimmest association came from the legend that Judas hanged himself from an Elder. This story persists in the fungus named *Auricularia auricula-judae*, originally translated 'Judas' Ear', later known as 'Jew's Ear' (though in these more politically correct times 'Jelly Ear' is sometimes substituted). These odd, brownish fungi, with very much the texture of the upper part of an ear, are quite good to eat, and are found in autumn growing out of the cracks in Elder bark.

and some of the new purple-leaved selections are extremely effective when kept cut right back to fit into herbaceous borders.

Solanum dulcamara (Bittersweet)

SOLANACEAE *(Nightshade family)*

This common and attractive climber is frequently accused in the gardening press of being a vicious, deadly species, to be destroyed on sight. This is unfair. All members of the Solanaceae, in the same family as potatoes, need to be treated with respect, as various parts of various plants can contain some powerful chemicals, and there are two native plants in the family which contain serious poisons. *Atropa belladonna* (Deadly Nightshade – the real thing) and *Hyoscyamus niger* (Henbane) both contain hyoscyamine, and in their early medical use must have killed quite as often as they cured. The drug still has a valuable use in some stomach sedatives, but is more notorious for being the poison Dr Crippen used to murder his wife. These two plants both have interesting and dramatic looks, so are obviously not recommended for any garden where they might catch the attention of uninformed children, and Henbane should be handled with gloves in case juice enters a cut, but no plant is going to jump up to attack a sensible adult gardener! Bittersweet (also called Woody Nightshade) is anyway a much less toxic species, and makes a pleasant addition to a mixed hedge. The flowers are perky little purple and yellow pagoda shapes, and these are followed in autumn by abundant red berries, which could be poisonous if eaten in large quantity, but are so bitter and unpleasant at first nibble that this would be extremely unlikely. The various red berries in native hedges are part of the autumn landscape, and demonizing this particular plant comes from the modern fear of nature, rather than from any historic bad reputation.

Hedge necklace – Black Bryony berries.

Tamus communis (Black Bryony)

DIOSCOREACEAE *(Black Bryony family)*

Although this twining plant is common in Britain south of about Durham, and its wreathing stems of red berries show up in autumn looking from a distance quite like those of White Bryony or Bittersweet, it is actually a long way from either of these look-alikes in the scheme of botanical relationships. In effect, White Bryony is close to cucumbers (hairy with quite broad leaves), and Bittersweet is close to capsicums (the pixy-hat flowers shaped like those of tiny potatoes), but Black Bryony comes between the agaves and the orchids! This rather exotic placing is borne out if you look at the plant closely, because the stems and heart-shaped leaves are fascinatingly smooth, looking almost oiled when fresh and deep green. Robert Gathorne-Hardy (1961) thought it had 'the sort of leaf which gothic sculptors might have carved'. The trailing stems die off as the berries ripen, so the vines droop in the most graceful wreaths and necklaces over hedges and shrubs.

Part of the view – Gorse (Furze) in Co. Wexford.

Ulex europaeus (Gorse)

FABACEAE, syn. PAPILIONACEAE –
(Pea family)

County flower of Belfast

There used to be a saying, 'When the Gorse is out of blossom, kissing's out of fashion' – in other words, never! This ubiquitous shrub can be found with a few flowers in every month of the year, although the main season, when the glorious yellow flowers scent cliffs and heaths and hills with coconut and honey, is around April. Gorse (also commonly called Furze or Whin, remembered in place names such as Fersfield and Whinfell) used to be an important subsistence resource for country people. It was used for rough roof thatching, for kindling, for strengthening fences, even for animal food – both horses and donkeys can cleverly mumble it around in their mouths till the spines are harmless. In times and places when poverty was not too harsh, it became useful to the rich, because thickets of Gorse, often on slopes which were 'spare' because of being too steep to plough, could be left as coverts for game. It is really only since the middle of the last century that Gorse has been seen purely as a pest, to be bulldozed out of many parts of the landscapes it has defined for so long. It is possible, however, now that the grabbing of marginal land for conifer plantations has slowed down, that Gorse may make a return.

There are two other native species of *Ulex: U. gallii* (Western Gorse) and *U. minor* (Dwarf Gorse), both of which flower in the autumn. Dwarf Gorse is really only found in scattered areas of southern England, and is less conspicuous than its relatives, but Western

Even better in its double form: Gorse in full flower.

Gorse covers large parts of Exmoor for instance, flowering with *Erica cinerea* (Bell Heather) and *Calluna vulgaris* (Ling) in an outrageous blaze of egg-yolk yellow and purple. In Ireland the Co. Wexford branch of the GAA (Gaelic Athletic Association, Cumann Lúthchleas Gael) proudly wear 'the purple and gold' as their colours for both hurling and Gaelic football, and these flowers really represent the county, featuring in traditional songs and in more modern literature such as Colm Tóibín's novel *The Heather Blazing*. However, the common Gorse is the most garden-worthy of the three species, always available from landscape firms, and a good addition to a mixed native hedge (planted on the sunny side). There is a wonderful selection with double flowers, 'Flore Pleno' AGM, which has the fragrance of the wild plant but naturally gives an even more wonderful show. Gorse is not long-lived,

and does not respond well to pruning attempts, so it is best enjoyed for a few years in a hedge or shrubbery, or on a grassy bank, and then cut or pulled out when it begins to look leggy (removal is usually surprisingly easy) and replaced.

Ulmus glabra (Wych Elm)

ULMACEAE *(Elm family)*

The great Elm trees which once characterized the English landscape (particularly since the Enclosures of the eighteenth century) and the disastrous outbreak of Dutch Elm Disease in the 1970s are outside the scope of this book, except for one oddity, which is a delightful garden plant. The main British *Ulmus* species do still exist, usually as hedgerow suckers, but they are unable to grow beyond the size of a really small tree. Dutch Elm Disease is caused by a fungus (genus *Ophiostoma*) which is spread by a type of weevil (genus *Scolytus*, Bark Beetle). When trees reach a certain size the bark begins to have splits and crevices, which let the beetles carry the fungus spores into the trunk. Of the native elms *U. glabra* (Wych Elm) is the most disease resistant, but *U. minor* agg. (Small-leaved Elm) and *U. procera* (English Elm) succumb while quite small. Elms have frequently hybridized, and there are many varieties, some with very complicated genetic histories. Among them is a charming little tree which belongs to a group of hybrids known as *U. × hollandica* (which are generally *U. glabra × U. minor* but may have a number of other strains in the mix). This is 'Jacqueline Hillier', a slow-growing shrub originally found in a Birmingham garden and named at Hillier's Arboretum. The branches grow close together, sticking up at quite a sharp angle and giving the bare shrub a lovely 'fish-bone' silhouette, still visible when the small leaves are on. It seldom reaches more than 2m, and that takes time, so the danger of the bark ever splitting is small. The shrub may sucker, but is quite easily managed and kept to one trunk, looking graceful and unusual in a shrubbery or grown as a specimen shrub.

Autumn leaves of the Wayfaring Tree.
INSET: **Red berries ripen to black.**

Viburnum lantana (Wayfaring Tree); *V. opulus* (Guelder Rose)

CAPRIFOLIACEAE *(Honeysuckle family)*

This is a large and popular genus. Many gardeners love *Viburnum* just as they love *Daphne*, collecting and growing as many species as possible, and again there are two natives to consider. In early spring

Daphne laureola (Spurge Laurel) and *D. mezereum* (Mezereon) are desirable at a time when more exotic species have not come into growth. Wayfaring Tree and Guelder Rose feature in summer, when they flower, and more importantly with their autumn berries. They are both quite common as hedge plants and in scrub, usually on calcareous soils, though Guelder Rose tolerates and even enjoys quite damp soil and a little shade. Wayfaring Tree is found in England and Wales up to about Lincolnshire, but Guelder Rose grows throughout most of Britain and Ireland.

Guelder Rose has glorious red berries.

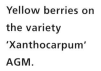

Yellow berries on the variety 'Xanthocarpum' AGM.

The genus name *Viburnum* may have old links to Latin *via*, meaning 'road', because these shrubs were familiar to travellers on highways.

Wayfaring Tree is actually a bush, not a tree, with felted bark and roundish leaves. In summer it has flat heads of off-white flowers, looking not unlike a dense Cow Parsley umbel but held on stiff twigs, and adds shape and focus to a mixed hedge. The berries are interesting rather than spectacular. Small and narrow, they sit upright on the 'plate' of the flower head, turning from green to red, and then ripening to black. Often at least two of the colours will be visible at once on the same head. Grigson (1958) tells us: 'You can eat the fruit when they go black, with no ill consequence, but also, I think, no great pleasure'; but he adds, 'it is a shrub to admire for autumn effects'. Leaf colour can be lovely, if the hedge is reasonably sunny, with red tones looking particularly good with the

clear gold of Field Maple and the dark purple of Dogwood. As a footnote, the leaves were formerly used to
make a black hair dye.

Guelder Rose is a showier bush, with flat bright-
white heads in summer, and spectacular drooping
bunches of translucent scarlet autumn berries. The
flowers consist of broad, sterile outer florets, which
are white, surrounding inconspicuous little dingy fertile flowers. Leaves and twigs are smooth, the leaves
much greener than those of Wayfaring Tree. The
beloved 'Snowball Bush' of gardens is a double form,
V. opulus 'Roseum' AGM, known to Gerard in the sixteenth century, and widely available now (though of
course it will not produce berries). The berries are glorious – much beloved of birds of course, but giving a
wonderful show before winter brings avine hunger.
The leaves too can become really red, so the whole
bush blazes. This species can grow to quite a generous size if you want it as a specimen shrub, and a large
bush can be very effective near a pond, but it is
equally quite happy in a trimmed hedge. Garden
selections include smaller forms, and there are variations in both leaf and berry colour. It is thought that
the odd name properly belongs to the double form,
which may first have been cultivated near Guelder on
the Holland/Germany border centuries ago, being
introduced to Britain as a gardener's novelty.

Striking silhouettes – Mistletoe on a large poplar.

Viscum album (Mistletoe)

VISCACEAE (*Mistletoe family*)

County flower of Herefordshire

There could be no better or more thought-provoking
plant than Mistletoe to provide the final note of the
natural year. This whole family (which extends world-
wide, with each genus as weird as the others) is
deeply fascinating and mysterious. Books and websites concerned with European mythology and folklore are full of stories about its powers, and other
'mistletoes' found as far apart as Japan, New Guinea
and South Africa have similar tales and beliefs surrounding them. Quite apart from the Roman author

and naturalist Pliny the Elder (AD 23–79) who wrote
about Druids and Mistletoe and Sacred Oak Groves in
his 'encyclopaedic' book , making the plant famous
in that context, the whole appearance and behaviour
of Mistletoe is remarkable, and lends itself to every
kind of magical interpretation. There are the leaves
that curve at the end of twigs into a crescent shape,
suggesting many symbolic meanings; the strange
translucent white midwinter berries and the even
stranger spring flowers, which open like little mouths
set in the stems; there is its apparently parasitic
growth on important trees – great oaks, golden
apples; and the dramatic appearance of large Mistle-

Always mysterious – Mistletoe in fruit on an apple tree.

toe balls silhouetted against winter skies. Mistletoe actually absorbs much of its own food like any other green plant, and mostly uses the tree to anchor itself, which accounts for the host usually being perfectly healthy even after years of 'having its life sucked out'. The plant seems to have had a special place in popular consciousness throughout history, and naturally has ancient associations with winter festivals, while the rather frog-spawn-like appearance of the berries made fertility associations likely. The kissing habit may have been degraded by many modern office parties, but it has distinguished and fascinating ancient origins. Mistletoe was also believed to have healing properties, and some of these are interesting because they are being re-examined in modern times. It was thought in the Middle Ages to revive people (or even bring them to life again) after severe epileptic seizures, and is known to have been used in complementary medicine centuries later as an anti-spas-

modic and against high blood pressure. It still appears in herbal treatments for these conditions. More importantly now another of its historic uses is a focus for research. A number of mistletoes contain chemicals called lectins. These are powerful, and dangerous if misused (ricin, extracted from castor oil plants, is a restricted substance under anti-terrorism laws), but may prove to be effective against some cancer cells, echoing the medieval belief that Mistletoe could cure tumours.

The 'frequently-asked question' from interested gardeners is of course how to get it to grow at home. The Internet abounds with advertisements for 'starter packs', but there is no reason not to use the berries off your Christmas bunch. It is frequently distributed by birds which eat the pulp of the berries and then wipe the sticky residue (containing the hard seed) off their beaks onto nearby branches. The same can be done by hand, pushing berries into cracks and crevices in bark where they will stay in place, but also 'see daylight'. Grigson (1958) makes it all sound very simple, sticking berries on branches, though he suggests

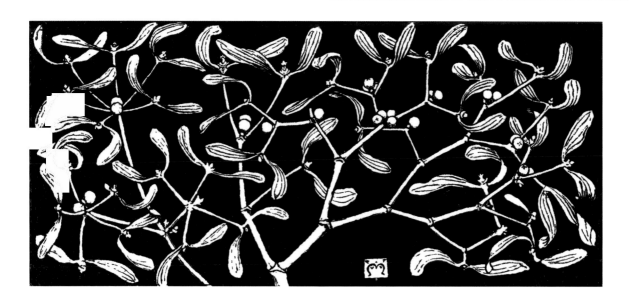

tying a strip of thinly woven material round the places to hold the seed secure, and also (sensibly) to remind you where it is. There are records of 'grow your own' experiments from the eighteenth century, trying different host trees. Ironically, the oak is the most difficult to start a colony on. The commonest hosts are apples, hawthorns, ornamental *Prunus* and *Sorbus* (in fact it seems fond of Rosaceae); limes and poplars (sometimes spectacularly); and there have been reports of plants on *Robinia* trees in parks and gardens. Our native Mistletoe seldom grows on evergreens, and although this does occur occasionally it is the effect of the green bunches on otherwise bare branches that looks so striking, and the plants proba-

bly need their winter light. Continental species, which grow in much higher ambient light levels, are more frequently found on evergreen hosts such as *Abies*. Botanists are usually interested in host plants, and local societies may have information. Mistletoe has had quite a high conservation profile, because modern losses of traditional orchards have threatened the guest as well as the host, so interested residents in country areas are usually aware of how 'their' Mistletoe is doing. It is hoped that the reviving interest in historic fruit varieties, and agri-environment schemes supporting traditional methods, may slow this decline.

GLOSSARY

acid
Soil with a pH value of 6.5 or lower.

adventitious
Refers to part of a plant occurring in an unusual location.

agg. (aggregatum)
One species name used as an aggregate to cover several plants in a closely related group.

alien
Not native, introduced by humans.

alkaline
Soils with a pH value of 7.5 or above (see also calcareous).

annual
A plant that completes its life-cycle within one year.

anther
The part of a flower stamen producing pollen, held on a stalk-like filament. The stamen is the cover name for all the parts.

aquatic
A plant living in water (free-floating, submerged or rooted on the bottom).

axis
The stem on which parts such as flowers or leaves are arranged.

back-cross
A hybrid plant crossing with one of its parents.

base-rich
A calcareous soil with a high calcium carbonate or magnesium carbonate content.

bicoloured
With two distinct colours.

biennial
A plant completing its life-cycle in two years, with vegetative growth in the first year, flowers in the second.

binomial
The botanical name of a plant, comprising two words. The first word (the generic name) identifies its genus. The second word (the specific epithet) gives the species name.

bloom
(a) Flower.
(b) Fine, waxy bluish or greyish coating.

bract
Modified leaf at base of flower or floret, often small or scale-like.

calcareous
Soils with high calcium carbonate (chalk) or magnesium carbonate content. Also called limy or base-rich.

calcicole
A plant thriving on calcareous soils.

calyx
Collective term for the sepals which form the outer whorl of the perianth under the flower petals.

capsule
A dry fruit containing seeds, which splits to shed.

cladode
A branch taking on the form and functions of a leaf.

clay
Heavy, very fertile, moisture-retentive soil.

cleistogamous
Flowers that self-pollinate without opening.

coppice
To prune trees or shrubs nearly to ground level (sometimes annually) to encourage strong new growth. The main woody growing point is the stump or stool.

corm
Swollen, solid underground stem, producing growth but not a bulb. Replacing itself annually.

cultivar (short for cultivated variety)
Plant raised or selected in cultivation, which remains distinct and stable.

dead-head
To remove spent flower heads, preventing seeding and encouraging continued growth.

deciduous
Shedding leaves or petals at the end of the growing season.

dehiscence
The process of splitting open at maturity.

denizen
A plant established in a garden but not deliberately planted.

dioecious
With male and female flowers on different plants.

dormant
Resting, without active growth.

double
Flowers having more petals than the normal wild form, and usually no anthers, or very few.

drainage
Movement of excess water through soil. Can be enhanced by adding e.g. gravel. 'Good' or 'sharp' drainage allows moisture to drain freely.

drupe
A fleshy fruit containing one or more hard-coated seeds.

environment
Sum total of external influences affecting a plant.

epiphytic
Growing on another plant without taking nutrients from it.

escape
A former garden plant which has become self-sufficient and established outside.

evergreen
A plant keeping (most of) its leaves throughout the year.

f. (forma, form)
A variant of a species distinguished by a minor character such as leaf or flower colour. (See also var.)

family
Category in plant classification, encompassing genera (singular genus) which share general appearance and technical characteristics.

filament
The thread-like stem of an anther (occasionally used of hair-like structures).

flore pleno
With a double flower.

floret
Tiny individual flower within a dense inflorescence.

garden origin
Refers to a plant artificially bred or selected, not found in the wild.

genus (pl. genera, adj. generic)
Category in plant classification, between family and species, encompasses species sharing many characteristics. The name of the genus in a scientific plant name always has a capital letter (e.g. *Bellis perennis*). (See also binomial.)

glaucous
With a greyish-blue bloom.

ground cover
Low layer of vegetation, often under shrubs or trees. Dense, low-growing herbaceous plantings to suppress weeds.

habit
The form and characteristic appearance of a mature plant.

habitat
The normal location for a plant to grow in, determined by the amount of light and water available, the type of soil, and the average weather conditions.

**hemi-parasite
(half-parasite, semi-parasite)**
A plant that gets some of its
nourishment from a host plant.

herb
(a) A plant used in cooking or
medicine.
(b) Botanically, any herbaceous
(non-woody) plant. A 'herb-rich
turf' in a meadow has
many flowering plants as well as
grasses.

humus
Decomposed organic matter in
soil. Rotted garden compost or
leaf-mould will add humus to soil,
increase bacterial activity and
improve structure.

inflorescence
The arrangement of flowers on a
single axis; a flower cluster.

introduction
See naturalized.

in situ
In the original or natural position
or habitat.

invasive
Used to describe a vigorous plant
that quickly overwhelms more
delicate neighbours and takes over
bare soil.

karst
Bare, weathered and fissured
limestone area.

latex
A juice produced from cut stems
or leaves of some plants (e.g.
spurges), usually milky, sometimes
orange.

monoecious
Having male and female flowers
on the same plant.

mulch
Layer of material spread on soil
around plants, such as leaf-mould
or garden compost.

native (indigenous)
Naturally growing wild in certain
areas.

naturalized
Established and looking wild, but
actually introduced from another
region or country.

neutral
Soils with pH value of around 7.0,
neither acid nor alkaline.

node (joint)
The point on a stem which
produces one or more leaves.

nutrients
Minerals and other substances
needed for healthy growth.

open pollination
Natural pollination by wind or
insects.

pedicel
Stalk of an individual flower.

peduncle
Stalk of a group of flowers.

perianth
Collective term for sepals and
petals of a whole flower.

perennial
Plant (usually non-woody) that
lives for a number of years.

pH
A measure of acidity or alkalinity,
used to assess soils. The scale goes
from 1 (extremely acid) to 15
(extremely alkaline). Garden soils
are often 5.5–7.5. (See acid,
alkaline, neutral.)

photosynthesis
The chemical process by which
green plants use sunlight to
convert carbon dioxide and water
into carbohydrates.

pollen
The dust-like grains containing the
male reproductive cells of a flower,
released from anthers.

pollard
To manage tree growth by cutting
branches back hard to the main
trunk, usually done at regular
intervals.

pollination
Transfer of pollen to stigma, of the
same flower (self-pollination) or
others (open pollination). Pollen
may be moved by insects, animals,
wind or water (or, in the garden,
by hand).

prostrate (procumbent)
Species or variety of plant with
stems growing flat to the ground.

raceme
Inflorescence with short-stalked flowers radiating off a single, unbranched stem (the axis), the youngest flowers at the tip.

rhizome
A root-like stem lying horizontally on or under the soil surface, producing buds or shoots and adventitious roots (which are not part of the main root system).

rosette
A dense, circular cluster of leaves at the central stem base of a plant, growing at ground level.

runner
A spreading stem, growing above or below ground to produce new shoots or plantlets away from the main plant.

scree
Unstable rock and gravel slopes below cliffs, usually rather dry.

section
A subdivision of a genus, applied to plants which have close similarities.

scrub
Habitat with bushes and small trees, often on poor or neglected soils.

self-pollination
Means by which a flower can pollinate its own female organ. An emergency technique which denies genetic additions.

self-seed
To regenerate in a garden without human intervention.

semi-double
Having an intermediate number of petals, between a basic single flower and a real double.

sepal
A single segment of a calyx – usually small and leaf-like, occasionally coloured.

sharp drainage
Free and fast movement of excess water through soil.

sp. (plural spp.)
Abbreviation of species.

species (plural species)
The basic unit of plant classification, used for closely related plants that breed true in the wild, and have stable, recognizable differences from similar groups. The descriptive specific epithet is the second word of a binomial, and is written with a lower case initial letter. (See also binomial, genus.)

sport
A name for a variant plant or shoot produced by a genetic change or mutation. Variegations often arise like this.

ssp. (plural sspp.)
Abbreviation of subspecies.

stamen
A male sex organ, usually including an anther and filament.

stolon
A lateral stem or runner growing along at ground level, rooting at the nodes to produce new plants.

stool
The stumps left after cutting woody growth to ground level (coppicing), or for the cutting activity itself.

subshrub
A low-growing but woody-stemmed plant, or a woody-based plant with soft stem growth.

subsoil
The layer below topsoil, usually of poor quality, commonly found around new buildings.

subspecies (plural subspecies)
A plant classification used to distinguish plants within a species which have slight but stable differences from the main type.

sucker
A subterranean shoot, usually coming from roots rather than the main crown of a plant.

syn.
Abbreviation of synonym. Another name for a taxon, now out of date.

syn.*
Used in this book to identify certain new usages.

taproot
A strongly developed main root; any side roots are much smaller.

taxon (plural taxa)
A unit of classification covering all ranks, e.g. *Bellis perennis* (species), *Bellis* (genus), *Asteraceae* (family).

taxonomy
Scholastic botany dealing with the identification, classification and naming of plants.

temperate
Climate zones between the subtropics and the polar circles, with distinct seasons, few temperature extremes, and rainfall throughout the year (as in the UK).

true (true-breeding)
Plants which replicate the characteristics of their parents when raised from seed.

tuber
Underground root or stem swollen with stored food reserves.

tunic
The dry papery or fibrous covering of a bulb or corm.

umbel
An inflorescence with all the minor flower stalks (pedicels) growing from a single point at the top of the main stalk (the peduncle). Umbels can be flat-topped (as in the carrot family) or rounded (as in the large decorative *Allium* cultivars).

understorey
Vegetation layer of shrubs and saplings growing between the tree canopy and ground cover in a wood.

variation
Differences from the normal appearance or behaviour of a plant, which may be caused by the environment or a genetic change.

variety (in science varietas)
Term used (particularly in gardens) to designate a group of plants which differs in colour or form from the basic species. Ranks between subspecies and forma.

var.
Abbreviation of variety (plural vars.)

RECOMMENDED SUPPLIERS

Arne Herbs,
Limeburn Nurseries, Limeburn Hill,
Chew Magna, Bristol BS40 8QW
Telephone: (01275) 333399
Email: arneherbs@aol.com
Website: www.arneherbs.co.uk

Birkheads Secret Gardens,
Birkheads Lane, Nr Sunniside,
Newcastle upon Tyne NE16 5EL
Telephone: (01207) 232262
Email:
birkheadsnursery@gmail.com
Website:
www.birkheadssecretgardens.co.uk

Chew Valley Trees,
Winford Road, Chew Magna,
Bristol BS40 8HJ
Telephone: (01275) 333752
Website:
www.chewvalleytrees.co.uk

Landlife Wildflowers Ltd,
National Wildflower Centre,
Court Hey Park, Liverpool L16 3NA
Telephone: (0151) 737 1819
Email: gill@landlife.org.uk
Website: www.wildflower.org.uk

**Lodge Farm Plants and
Wildflowers**
Case Lane, Fiveways, Hatton,
Warwickshire CV35 7JD
Telephone: (01926) 484649
Email:
lodgefarmplants@btinternet.com
Website:
www.lodgefarmplants.com

Mires Beck Nursery,
Low Mill Lane, North Cave,
Brough, East Riding,
Yorkshire HU15 2NR
Telephone: (01430) 421543
Email: admin@miresbeck.co.uk
Website: www.miresbeck.co.uk

Saith Ffynnon Wildlife Plants,
Saith Ffynnon Farm, Whitford,
Holywell, Flintshire, North Wales
CH8 9EN
Telephone: (01352) 711198
Email: jan@7wells.org
Website: www.7wells.co.uk

Poyntzfield Herb Nursery,
Nr Balblair, Black Isle, Dingwall,
Ross-shire, Scotland IV7 8LX
Telephone: (01381) 610352
Email: info@poyntzfieldherbs.co.uk
Website:
www.poyntzfieldherbs.co.uk

Really Wild Flowers,
H.V. Horticulture Ltd,
55 Balcombe Road, Haywards
Heath, West Sussex RH16 1PE
Telephone: (01444) 413376
Email: info@reallywildflowers.co.uk
Website:
www.reallywildflowers.co.uk

Shipton Bulbs,
Y Felin, Henllan Amgoed,
Whitland, Carmarthenshire,
Wales SA34 0SL
Telephone: (01994) 240125
Email: bluebell@zoo.co.uk
Website: www.bluebellbulbs.co.uk

**Water Meadow Nursery
and Herb Farm**,
Cheriton, Nr Alresford,
Hampshire SO24 0QB
Telephone: (01962) 771895
Email: plantaholic@onetel.com
Website: www.plantaholic.co.uk

USEFUL ORGANIZATIONS

All of the organizations listed deal with wild plant recording, have regional representatives and membership activities, and are approachable sources of valuable knowledge. Flora locale also runs a Native Seed Forum.

Botanical Society of the British Isles (BSBI),
The Botany Department,
The Natural History Museum,
Cromwell Road, London SW7 5BD
Website: www.bsbi.org.uk

Flora Locale,
Postern Hill Lodge, Marlborough,
Wiltshire SN8 4ND
Telephone: 01672 515723
Website: www.floralocale.org

Plantlife,
14 Rollestone Street, Salisbury,
Wiltshire SP1 1DX
Telephone: 01722 342370
Website: www.plantlife.org.uk

The Wild Flower Society,
Membership Secretary,
43 Roebuck Road, Rochester, Kent ME1 1UE
Website: www.thewildflowersociety.com

BIBLIOGRAPHY

Bailes, C., and Andrews, S., *Hollies for Gardeners* (Timber Press, 2006)

Brickell, C. (ed.), *The Royal Horticultural Society A–Z Encyclopedia of Garden Plants* (Dorling Kindersley, 1996)

Cubey, J. et al (eds.), *RHS Plant Finder 2010–2011* (Dorling Kindersley, 2010) (Updated annually.)

Ekwall, E. (ed.), *The Concise Oxford Dictionary of English Place-names* (4th edition, OUP, 1960)

Fearnley-Whittingstall, J., *Ivies* (Random House, 1992)

Gathorne-Hardy, R., *The Native Garden* (Thomas Nelson & Sons Ltd, 1961)

Greenwood, P. and Halstead, A., *The Royal Horticultural Society – Pests and Diseases* (Dorling Kindersley, 1997)

Grigson, G., *The Englishman's Flora* (Readers' Union, 1958)

Grigson, G., *A Dictionary of English Plant Names* (Allen Lane, 1973)

Hickey, M. and King, C., *The Cambridge Illustrated Glossary of Botanical Terms* (CUP, 2000)

Ingwersen, W.T., *Wild Flowers in the Garden* (The Garden Book Club, n.d. [1952])

Lloyd, C., *Foliage Plants* (Collins, 1973)

Lloyd, C., *Garden Flowers* (Cassell & Co., 2000)

Mabey, R., *Flora Britannica* (Sinclair-Stevenson, 1996)

Phillips, R. and Rix, M., *Shrubs* (Macmillan, 1994)

Robinson, W., *The Wild Garden* (John Murray, 1870, Century Publishing Co. Ltd, 1983)

Stace, C.A. (ed.), *New Flora of the British Isles* (3rd edition, CUP, 2010)

Thomas, G.S., *Perennial Garden Plants* (J.M. Dent, 1976)

INDEX